The Scottish Football Book No 24

D0496355

THE SCOTTISH FOOTBALL BOOK NO 24

Edited by Hugh Taylor

Stanley Paul, London

Stanley Paul & Co Ltd
3 Fitzroy Square, London W1P 6 JD

An imprint of the Hutchinson Publishing Group

London Melbourne Sydney Auckland
Wellington Johannesburg and agencies
throughout the world

First published 1978

© Stanley Paul & Co Ltd 1978

Photographs © Martin Wright, Colorsport, Glasgow
Herald, Press Association, Derek Evans

Set in VIP Baskerville by Input Typesetting Ltd
Printed in Great Britain by The Anchor Press Ltd
and bound by Wm Brendon both of Tiptree, Essex.

ISBN 0 09 133901 4

Colour photographs: Scotland v Ireland (p.2 of colour
section) and Aberdeen v Partick Thistle (p.8) by
Martin Wright; Bobby Russell and Gordon Smith
(p.5) Sportapix; all others by Colorsport.

Frontispiece: Derek Johnstone of Rangers, Scotland's
Player of the Year, showing great form in the Scottish
Cup Final against Aberdeen.

CONTENTS

Aberdeen skipper Willie Miller ... a certainty for Scotland's next World Cup team.

Hibs' Bobby Smith ... one of Scotland's most versatile youngsters.

THE EDITOR SAYS...

Gregor Stevens, Motherwell . . . one of the most effective defenders in the country.

One of the most dramatic soccer seasons in years, that of 1977–78, was dominated by Scotland's success in qualifying for the World Cup in Argentina – and by Rangers.

Rangers won the treble of League Cup, Premier League and Scottish Cup. Aberdeen made a gallant bid to prevent Jock Wallace's magnificent team sweeping the boards – and did enough to prove that this season they will be the team to watch.

In other divisions, too, interest was at fever-heat right to the end.

And what a day Saturday 29 April 1978 turned out to be – the longest day of the season for six teams, as the footballing year pushed towards its enthralling climax.

In the Premier League, champagne flowed as Rangers beat Motherwell 2–0 at Ibrox to cruise to their thirty-seventh championship.

And there was joy at Tannadice as Dundee United swept into Europe and the UEFA Cup by beating Partick Thistle and joy too at Easter Road where a rejuvenated Hibernian drew with Aberdeen and earned their place in the UEFA tournament.

But for Celtic, for so long the pride of Scotland, the scourge of the Continentals, it was gloomy. They missed going into Europe for the first time in seventeen years. They needed a draw against St Mirren – but lost 3–1 at Love Street.

Drama all the way, also, in the First and Second Division. Hearts won by the only goal at Arbroath to accompany Morton, surprise packet of the season, into the Pre-

mier League. And Clyde became champions of the Second Division in their first season under manager Craig Brown and progress, with Raith Rovers their companions, into the First Division.

But it was Rangers' season – Rangers who, amazingly, had opened their League campaign with two defeats and were at the bottom of the Premier Division for a spell.

Manager Jock Wallace, however, put his faith in stylish, artistic football, and shrewd buys, such as Gordon Smith from Kilmarnock and Davie Cooper from Clydebank, finally paid off, although probably the Ranger of the year was the unknown Bobby Russell, thrust into the first team and developing into a young man with the genius of a John White or Jimmy Mason.

Certainly there had never been a wind-up to the season like that of 1977–78, with the championships up for grabs in all three leagues on the last day.

To me, the happiest note was the number of fine young players bursting through – Russell, Frank McGarvey of St Mirren, Andy Ritchie of Morton, Tommy Burns of Celtic, John McMaster of Aberdeen, Eamon Bannon of Hearts, Ian Clinging of Motherwell and so many more, showing that Scotland is still the most prolific football nursery of them all.

The season had shocks – but none bigger than the resignation of Rangers manager Jock Wallace soon after he had taken the club to the Scottish treble, because he felt 'unhappy' at Ibrox. Skipper John Greig took over as manager to the delight of the Rangers supporters.

And then there was a reshuffle at Parkhead with Jock Stein becoming a director and Billy McNeill moving from Aberdeen to take over as manager of Celtic. Alec Ferguson, sacked by St Mirren, became the new boss at Aberdeen.

Now let's kick off again with yet another edition of the *Scottish Football Book*. I hope you enjoy it.

Hugh Taylor

Frank McGarvey of St Mirren ... the nippy attacker the big English clubs want.

WORLD CUP BLUES

The autumn leaves that fell sadly over the beautiful Mendoza Stadium in Argentina weren't a wreath for yet another World Cup funeral. They symbolized tears for yet another what-might-have-been, and I didn't know that cold evening of 11 June 1978 (which is autumn in that part of South America) whether to cheer or cry.

Scotland had just beaten Holland, who made it to the final only to lose to the host country, Argentina; and it was an epic victory. Once again Scotland had played with power and passion. They had the skill and the poise, the artistry and the all-out action, the pattern and the will to prove that they could have been a fine World Cup side, a side to bring pride to the nation.

They had decisively defeated one of the best footballing countries in the tournament and had the usually imperturbable Dutch jittery. They held the game in their hands for practically ninety minutes and they were within an ace of bringing off the miracle of this football century – a triumph by the three clear goals they needed to qualify over the giants.

I will never forget that sixty-eighth minute when the courageous Archie Gemmill scored the brilliant goal that made it 3-1. Scotland were well on top, the Argentinian crowd were right behind them, yelling for a Scottish victory, baying abuse at the boring disorganized Dutch.

Battle of the giants. Scotland's Joe Jordan and Holland's Rudi Krol clash in the World Cup.

It didn't last, of course. The pace was too hot, the endeavour too grim, the inspiration impossible to sustain for ninety minutes. Holland proved they had pride, were still a splendid team. And the magnificent Johnny Rep turned the glorious Technicolor of Mendoza into drab grey for Scotland with one of his fantastic goals to make it 3-2 . . . and just when Scotland looked like adding another goal to that 3-1 total and making the next World Cup section for the first time.

So Scotland went home early. Their heads were high, though. For they proved they had the skill to play with the best, with performances from Gemmill, Bruce Rioch, the brave Joe Jordan, Martin Buchan and Tom Forsyth which will be talked about in Argentina in admiring, sibilant Spanish for years to come.

But still I cried. For this was the same old Scotland, the same old World Cup story. Why couldn't Scotland have played like that in the opening games which were vital – and in which Scotland were again a shambles? Why were we once again out of a World Cup on goal difference taking three points as Holland did to finish under the Dutch and Peru (who had five points) but with our goal difference 5-6 compared to Holland's 5-3?

Why did we have to ask the reasons why it's always too late for Scotland?

Sometimes, I felt again, we Scots border on insanity as far as football is concerned.

Behind me in the vast stadium, in the

wonderful setting of the foothills of the Andes, were a group of tartan-bedecked Scots ecstatic with joy, praising their heroes to the great blue sky above Mendoza – fans who only hours before were demanding vengeance, vowing they would never watch a Scotland match again.

Alas, that's Scotland – up and down like a runaway lift. What really made the difference to Scotland, what pinpointed previous mistakes in team selection, was the inclusion of Graeme Souness in the midfield. The dark, handsome Liverpool man made all the difference to the Scots. He has presence, arrogance, class, superb passing. He more than any made the team click – a cool, cold ruthless playmaker who got the best out of the gallant Jordan and the raiding Gemmill.

But why, why, why hadn't Scotland played like that against Peru and Iran? If they had, they would have been high and dry in the next round. Why hadn't manager Ally MacLeod realized that Don Masson had lost form? Why didn't Scotland have the cavalier Souness in from the start?

Perhaps there was too much euphoria at the start, too much optimism, with thousands of Scottish fans, who gave the squad a tremendous send-off from Hampden and Prestwick airport, convinced the team wouldn't only do well in Argentina . . . but would win the World Cup.

It all went wrong, however.

Scotland lost the vital opening match 3-1 to Peru in Cordoba – and the smirk that turned the swarthy face of Teofilo Cubillas into that of a *bandito* who has just robbed a bank of a hundred million *pesos* told the whole, dismal story of the World Cup humiliation.

Strutting proudly with his team-mates after the game, he took time off from signing autographs and receiving kisses from Peruvian girl supporters in red ponchos and blue jeans which seemed to be sprayed on to tight bottoms to tell me: '*Senor*, it was a *fiesta* for me, this match, a holiday. Maybe I

should be angry. Did Scotland think I am too old, that they ignored me?'

I don't know. All I do know is that the 29-year-old attacker who played in Europe with Oporto and Basle was given the freedom of a street as wide as Sauchiehall – and took full advantage of it.

That was Cubillas's business. My business was to inquire why Scotland played so unprofessionally, so naïvely in a game which once again made us the laughing stock of world football. I was near to tears as I thought afterwards about the match which showed that Scotland, despite all the pre-tournament ballyhoo, despite the money-building expertise in making the Scottish squad the wealthiest all-time losers in World Cup history, were still, if not quite the hapless amateurs who became clowns in Switzerland in 1954, innocents abroad compared with the knife-throwers and superb conmen of the rest of the nations.

Who was to blame for one of the most disgraceful defeats in a Scottish soccer history which has more Floddens than Bannockburns? The dirks were out again. Manager MacLeod blamed the players. The players felt there wasn't enough background information about Peru.

My view was that some of it went sour because the manager didn't know enough about Peru, whom he hadn't watched. Another reason was that too many players, of whom so much was expected, failed surprisingly.

But the brutal truth seemed to be that – despite excuses that if we had scored another goal, if we hadn't missed a penalty we would have won handsomely – Scotland's players still lacked the basic skills. . . . aye, even of countries like Peru.

Peru reminded me of the fine England teams of the Finney – Matthews – Mortensen era, slick, quick, strong. Not world beaters, however – as Argentina proved later on when they hammered them. That, of course, made Scotland's display all the

Little Asa Hartford, always busy, puts in a World Cup tackle.

more bitter. Scotland could have won, should have won. But, looking back at it calmly, now that the outrage, the disappointment was over, it was apparent our players were just not as good as those of other nations.

And the team lacked direction. Scotland could have done with a Billy Bremner who would have changed the pattern, would have had the Peruvians better marked, played a real captain's part when the Scots were falling apart. Scotland could have won the match twice. But they faltered both times after being on top. Obviously Don Masson and Bruce Rioch shouldn't have played. Obviously the injured Danny McGrain and Gordon McQueen were badly missed.

But the bitter truth is that despite all the idolizing of our boys in blue, despite that pathetic lap of honour after losing to England at Hampden, despite the fantastic farewell at Prestwick, despite exaggerated claims by those who should have known better that Scotland would win a medal if not the World Cup itself, we are not in the same class as the top ten in the competition. But how can you be professional when you miss a penalty – and give Peru all the confidence in the world?

It got worse.

Winger Willie Johnston was sent home in disgrace, having been found guilty of taking a stimulant. And Scotland hung her head in shame.

And for the game with Iran, the most important match Scotland had ever played, the match we had to win and win well to keep face with the rest of the world, the all-or-nothing clash with the men from the desert, manager MacLeod once again changed the style.

The manager put the accent on the buzz-buzz boys.

On parade were lads who get tore in. But it was a team without a pattern, a team without a playmaker. Out went Don Masson, who had been out of form. But who came in? Not another playmaker. Not Graeme Souness, the only other player in the depleted squad who had pretensions to world class. Ally had taken another gamble. He changed the style, demanding more aggression than he got against Peru, telling his men to smash in from the start.

Yet from the start of our World Cup campaign, from that magnificent first half against Czechoslavakia in Prague to Ken Dalglish's wonder goal at Anfield, the accent had been on the midfield, with two aggressive flank men in front of playmaker Masson.

How, we asked in the vale of tears that was Argentina that cold June day, could Tom Forsyth be dropped, how could a chance be taken with yet another central defence switch and, more than anything else, how could we take the field without a man of composure?

The middle men were bristling bantams – but it was like a Rangers team without a Baxter, a German side without a Beckenbauer. There was no blend in Scotland's new side. But the manager was adamant the players wouldn't be, as they were against Peru, frail flo'oers o' Scotland.

It seemed to me the new team Ally Mac Leod tried to build would take no prisoners,

would play with all the fury of a clan raid. But – was heart enough? I doubted it, for you just can't change a pattern midway through a World Cup campaign and hope to win. Again, however, everything had gone wrong for Scotland. The worst back in the tournament, everyone said, was Iran's Bahram Novodate. And Scotland were without Willie Johnston, back home in disgrace, a winger who would have shone against Novodate.

We all felt, too, that while Iran were not the greatest they were probably the worst team Scotland could have encountered at a tragic time for Scottish soccer. They were spoilers, more likely to get a 0-0 draw against the best in the world rather than to beat Mexico, the worst of them all, by 1-0.

Could Scotland rise to the occasion?

No, they couldn't.

The final disaster of a World Cup that started with high hopes and ended on another familiar note of *tour-de-farce* came in Cordoba, with a meagre crowd of 15 000 laughing openly at a Scotland team held to a 1-1 draw by Iran, Cinderellas of football.

And Scotland couldn't even score against their undistinguished opponents. The score was an own goal by Eskandarian.

Indeed, Scotland were lucky even to salvage the match. All our fears were proved right. Scotland revealed themselves once again as a Brechin among the sophisticates of the world. There was, as we had thought, no pattern. There was no modern know-how. It was more like a playground runaround than a match in the World Cup.

Now and again the skilful, dusky Iranians contemptuously perfected pretty patterns that had our defence gasping. Now and again there were slick raids by Danaie-Fard and Parvin. Our attackers looked as though their real home was Glasgow Green.

It's a match I don't want to remember – a match even worse for Scotland than any disaster against England or Uruguay

I thought our worst World Cup was our

first in 1954. I was wrong. Argentina was even more dreadful – because we were kidded, because people who should have known better conned us into thinking we had a good side, a professional side and professionals at the top. Demanded by all who watched the shameful performance was a thorough investigation into what went wrong. Why had the Scottish style been changed once again? Why was there no play controller at the back? Why wasn't Derek Johnstone of Rangers, the top scorer, given a chance to try to solve the goal shortage problem?

Furious Scottish fans demanded to know why those people who were so good and so professional about making money for doing the best financial Scottish job since the Darien scheme, forgot that it is planning for and playing good football that should come first.

The players never got a chance to turn into a settled side. It's true they weren't good enough to win a World Cup but if Scotland had taken the opportunity to try to play in one style before the World Cup – as so many others did – we might have made a hit.

As the spirits of the fans drooped, they began to ask: If Scotland can't beat Iran, where are we? Scotland, they added sarcastically, should stick to opening more and more shops, appointing at football's expense more and more commercial managers to bring in the big perks, composing songs of praise and jumping on the bandwagon of sidelines . . . instead of doing the real job, finding out about the opposition, deciding on a style, blending the team and trying to build a club side.

And so it was a sad farewell by Scotland to Argentina, farewell to taxis every one of which seemed to be driven by a Fangio, farewell to the friendliest people on earth, so many of whom took the Scots to their hearts and were genuinely sorry we went out of the World Cup in such a humiliating manner,

farewell to Cordoba, Alta Gracia and Mendoza and 'investigative' reporters who turned the sipping of a beer by a Scot into the swilling of a cask of whisky, farewell to the saddest, most dismal World Cup of them all, more wretched than the fiasco of 1954, the amateurish preparations of 1958 and the ill-starred but gallant exhibition of 1974.

More wretched because Scotland's fine play against Holland revealed that the team, properly handled, had the ability, the skill and the courage to have done really well in Argentina.

I felt, however, that manager MacLeod, a likeable man, a man who got the whole country behind the team with his enthusiasm and his magnificent public relations, executed himself in public in front of the San Francisco hotel in Mendoza under the shadow of the snow-capped Andes foothills when he held his last press conference.

He inferred some reporters had put his team under severe pressure, nobly defended his players, who had obviously been upset by some of the stories sent home, by saying they were the best behaved and best disciplined pool he had ever known, and that no other country had trained harder or better than Scotland.

You had to admire the guts of the man, a pale shadow, however, of the bouncing extrovert who had led Scotland all those miles over the Atlantic . . . to tragedy and disaster and, in the end, a triumph against Holland.

But he stood accused of making mistakes, of making poor team selections, of failing to motivate the players and of changing the pattern too often. Perhaps his trouble was that he had promised too much, was deceived by his own publicity and lacked the world-wide experience for the job.

The players, despite that glorious victory over Holland, were by no means blameless. There were no wild parties, no serious drinking. Of that I'm sure. Long before Scotland arrived in Argentina, the locals were talking about our reputation and the imagination of some of their journalists ran riot during the stay at remote Alta Gracia.

Still, the win over Holland must not blind us to the problems which arose, the letdowns and lack of real professionalism, the brutal truth that Scottish temperament seems fated to make certain we can never win a World Cup because our players just do not have the iron will or military monk discipline of those who are real contenders.

They become discontented, feel homesick, fail to train as strenuously as others, perhaps take a drink. It's the Scottish nature, the Scottish way of life. There's no way it will ever be changed.

Poor MacLeod took tremendous stick. But who would have done better? Who can turn happy-go-lucky Scottish soccer warriors into dedicated men of steel? We are, unfortunately, the great inconsistents of world football.

For instance, it was easy to spill tartan tears again in Cordoba soon after Scotland left – for you felt like crying as you listened to noisy, jubilant Dutch supporters parading the narrow streets of the old city, assuring the smiling Argentinians that Holland were certainties to win the World Cup.

For Holland were back on top of the soccer world with the greatest victory of the tournament so far against Austria. Yet only a few days before it was the Dutch who were sobbing into their duty-free gin they had brought from home, declaring Holland were finished, sympathizing with the Scottish fans because they had seen Scotland beat their country with a fine display but were quitting the World Cup scene.

I wanted to say that if only Scotland had played against Peru and Iran as they did against Holland we would have been putting every penny in our sporrans on us to win the cup.

I wanted to say that we, too, would have

hammered Austria 5-1 as a greatly depleted Dutch side did. But might-have-beens – as I seem to have said before – are nightmare episodes in Scotland's football history.

For who's to say, when you recall our avalanching from triumph to tragedy like a demented skier, what our team would have done against Austria. We might have played even more badly than we did against Peru and Iran.

So all I can say is that our latest might-have-been, in a forlorn, wistful glance back to the World Cup, reveals to me the major blunder made.

The horrifying mistake was to experiment in the home championships, to change our pattern. It took too long to find it again in the actual tournament and when we did – and succeeded so well against Holland – it was too late. We had been the blunderers, the babes against Peru and Iran.

But the toughest job in the world is undoubtedly that of a manager of a country playing in the top tournament. You must feel sorry for them. The strain is unbelievable. I sipped a planter's punch with grim-visaged Claudio Coutinho of Brazil, who seemed to have turned into an old man since the tournament began – a complete stranger from the smiling, straight-backed army officer I had interviewed in Rio de Janeiro only a year before. No wonder, though, his face was a map of despair. He had been sacked once in the tournament, then reinstated. But he knew Brazil must win the cup – they didn't, although they didn't lose a game – otherwise he would join, in some football desert, the foreign legion of former managers. He did, too, going to the United States.

Then, though, he was telling me about his troubles. 'The whole thing,' he said wearily, 'about being the manager of a

It's that man, Joe Jordan, again. The tall striker was one of the few Scottish heroes in Argentina.

world cup team is that you have to be 100 per cent every day of your life. That may seem simple to say. But how many people are even 100 per cent once a year? Very few. A manager cannot slip. He must be 100 per cent and he must make sure his players are 100 per cent, too.

'Not easy, *senor*, not easy, I assure you.'

Then he added that he felt sorry for Ally MacLeod and Scotland. 'The reason you went out,' he said, 'is that *Senor* MacLeod did not realize the great truth of the World Cup. He was never 100 per cent nor do I blame him. It is an impossible task. Impossible. But it must be done or .... pouff ... you're gone.'

Going on Couthino's theory, Scotland were only 30 per cent against Peru, 25 against Iran. Against Holland, perhaps 80 per cent. In training, 60 per cent. In discipline, 70 per cent. In morale after the match against Peru, zero per cent.

We just don't have the temperament to be at 100 per cent even for a week of the World Cup.

The saddest aspect of the World Cup was the disgrace of Willie Johnston, the West Bromwich Albion winger of whom so much was expected. Poor Willie. His white cheeks streaming with tears, holding his head in trembling hands, he muttered: 'Why must it always be me?' and you had to feel sorrow not shame for him as he was sent home.

Surrounded by sympathetic team-mates he sat dejectedly in the vast dining-room of the Sierras Hotel in Alta Gracia while outside SFA secretary Ernie Walker, in dark spectacles which symbolized Scotland's humiliation, emotionally issued a statement which ranked as the most abject ever made in a Scottish World Cup history packed with disaster.

Jordan always worried the Dutch in the World Cup battle in Argentina. Here you see him battling with Wildschut.

The statement said that Johnston had played against Peru under the influence of stimulant drugs, would be sent home, banned from ever playing for Scotland again and might have further disciplinary action taken against him.

It was Scotland's blackest day in football. And only then was Johnston realizing his career was in ruins.

He deserved to be punished. But the wee man from Fife who became one of the most fascinating wingers in soccer isn't a villain, isn't a cold-blooded schemer who felt drugs would make him play better.

His crime was that from which so many professional footballers suffer – stupidity. His ignorance, his failure to appreciate what he had done made me weep, for it was the complete unprofessionalism of it all that made Scotland the laughing stock of global football.

Johnston is anything but a dope addict. Off the field he is a quiet little man who has the odd lager. On the field, he is cheeky, often out of order but a tremendous competitor.

His trouble is that he is a highly nervous man. He suffers from hay fever. He has such palpitations before a game that often his legs come out in ugly blotches. At Ibrox he always took smelling salts before a game. Now with West Brom, he takes on doctor's prescription two tablets. Indeed, many English clubs tell their players to take these same stimulants before a match. They are anything but illegal in Britain. Willie took two before the Peru match. But he didn't tell anyone he had done so. So off home he had to go.

Poor Johnston. He's one of those great Scottish athletes to whom everything that shouldn't happens. He isn't a dirty player – but he chirps. He's a stormy petrel. His ordering-off record is unbelievable. He was sent off – for nothing – the year before in Argentina but no disciplinary action was taken against him.

And it had to happen again. 'Why must it always be me?' – repeats poor Willie time after time. And – why must it always be Scotland? I kept repeating.

Scotland again were the country to make the biggest headlines in a World Cup – and win nothing. But Johnston was more to be pitied than crucified.

His explanation was that he took two yellow tablets called Reactiva because he was feeling so low that at one stage he thought he wouldn't be able to play against Peru. He said he didn't think the tablets would have any effect on a doping test, so he didn't tell anyone, although he had been warned about the strict regulations concerning drugs in the World Cup.

As I said ... it's the stupidity of it all that makes you sigh for Scotland.

But the World Cup went on without Scotland, the great disappointment of the competition after reaching Argentina on a wave of passionate euphoria. And Ally MacLeod, loquacious, over-confident, flying over the Atlantic a hero, returned to Scotland as a figure of pathos. As someone said so succinctly: 'He failed to do his homework, went into the games with breezy ignorance and came a cropper.'

Scotland mourned. But they still watched matches on television. Disappointingly, the 1978 World Cup never became the great event it had been in such famous years as 1958, 1962 and 1970 when Brazil won with panache or 1974 when Holland and West Germany brought total football with all its versatility to a peak of perfection.

There weren't enough great players, for instance, and, unhappily, the two many people felt would be outstanding, Kenny Dalglish of Scotland and Reiner Bonhof of West Germany, never found top form.

The happiest feature of the competition was the enthusiasm of the Argentinians, so friendly, so ebullient. All through their country's matches, they filled the sky with a spectacular storm of torn-up paper and their uproar of celebration continued through the night in every city, town and village, the Avenidas Corrientes, Graz and San Martin – principal streets everywhere in Argentina – reverberating with sound. Rhythmic horn honking blared from miles-long jam-ups of flatulating vehicles. Inside, on top of and hanging from cars and trucks and motorbikes were thousands of happy Argentines, waving blue and white national flags and shouting, 'Ar –gen – tina! Ar – gen – tina!'

The locals were the *fiesta's* most exuberant guests.

In the end, Argentina beat Holland 3-1 after extra time in a final in which the brave Dutch were the better team.

Argentina, however, seemed pre-ordained to win. And some of the political aspects made one wonder why we worried so much about Scotland's disappointing showing. It seems to me there is no way now anyone but the host country can win. There's so much slanted against the opposition.

Anyhow, it was an undistinguished final, in which many neutrals wondered why the Italian referee had appeared on the field without a blue-and-white striped shirt and why Argentinian players took such a girlish attitude to physical contact.

Holland, I felt, never really had a chance but they were the best team in the 1978 tournament, although Argentina played with passion and attacking power.

And the consolation for Scotland remains: we could win the cup if we played as we played against Holland ... but all the time, that is.

Who now, though, expects the miracle of consistency to affect Scotland?

At last – joy for the Scottish fans in the World Cup in Mundoza

20

Scotland's teams in the 1978 World Cup were:

Against Peru in Cordoba, 3 June 1978: Rough, Kennedy, Forsyth, Burns, Buchan, Masson (Macari 70 mins), Hartford, Rioch (Gemmill 70 mins), Dalglish, Jordan, Johnston.
Peru: Quinoga, Diaz, Chumpitaz, Manzo, Duarte, Velasquez, Cuelto (Rojas 83 mins), Cubillas, Munante, La Rosa (Sotil 60 mins), Oblitas.
Referee: U. Eriksson, Sweden.

Against Iran in Cordoba, 7 June 1978: Rough, Jardine, Donachie, Burns, Buchan, Macari, Gemmill, Hartford, Dalglish (Harper 75 mins), Jordan, Robertson.
Iran: Hediazi, Nazari, Addolalu, Kazenani, Eskandarian, Parvin, Ghasen-Pour, Sadelii, Danaie-Fard, Fanaki, Jahani.
Referee: Youssou N'Diaye, Senegal.

Against Holland in Mendoza, 11 June 1978: Rough, Kennedy, Forsyth, Buchan, Donachie, Rioch, Souness, Gemmill, Hartford, Dalglish, Jordan.
Holland: Jongbloed, Suurbier, Krol, Portlivet, Rijsbergen, Neeskens, Jansen, W.van der Kerkhof, R. van der Kerkhof, Rep, Rensenbrink.
Referee: E. Linemayr, Austria.

GROUP 1

Hungary 1 (Csapo), **Argentina 2** (Luque, Bertoni), in Buenos Aires.
France 1 (Lacombe), **Italy 2** (Rossi, Zaccarelli), in Mar del Plata.
Argentina 2 (Passarella (pen), Luque), **France 1** (Platini), in Buenos Aires.
Italy 3 (Rossi, Bettega, Benetti), **Hungary 1** (A. Toth (pen)), in Mar del Plata.
Italy 1 (Bettega), **Argentina 0**, in Buenos Aires.
France 3 (Lopez, Berdolf, Rocheteau), **Hungary 1** (Zombori), in Mar del Plata.

GROUP 2

W. Germany 0, **Poland 0**, in Buenos Aires.
Tunisia 3 (Kaabi, Gommidh, Dhouib), **Mexico 1** (Vasquez (pen)), in Rosario.
Poland 1 (Lato), **Tunisia 0**, in Rosario.
Mexico 0, **W. Germany 6** (D. Muller, H. Muller, Rummenigge (2), Flohe (2)), in Cordoba.
Mexico 1 (Rangel), **Poland 3** (Boniek (2), Deyna), in Rosario.
Tunisia 0, **W. Germany 0**, in Cordoba.

GROUP 3

Spain 1 (Dani), **Austria 2** (Schachner, Krankl), in Buenos Aires.
Sweden 1 (Sjoberg), **Brazil 1** (Reinaldo), in Mar del Plata.
Austria 1 (Krankl (pen)), **Sweden 0**, in Buenos Aires.
Brazil 0, **Spain 0**, in Mar del Plata.
Sweden 0, **Spain 1** (Asensi), in Buenos Aires.
Brazil 1 (Roberto), **Austria 0**, in Mar del Plata.

GROUP 4

Peru 3 (Cueto, Cubillas (2)), **Scotland 1** (Jordan), in Cordoba.
Iran 0, **Holland 3** (Rensenbrink (3) (2 pen)), in Mendoza.
Scotland 1 (Eskandarian (og)), **Iran 1** (Danaie-Fard), in Cordoba.
Holland 0, **Peru 0**, in Mendoza.
Peru 4 (Velasquez, Cubillas (3)), **Iran 1** (Rowshan), in Cordoba.
Scotland 3 (Dalglish, Gemmill (2, 1 pen)), **Holland 2** (Rensenbrink (pen), Rep), in Mendoza.

GROUP 1

	P	W	D	L	F	A	P
Italy	3	3	0	0	6	2	6
Argentina ...	3	2	0	1	4	3	4
France	3	1	0	2	5	5	2
Hungary	3	0	0	3	3	8	0

GROUP 2

	P	W	D	L	F	A	P
Poland	3	2	1	0	4	1	5
W. Germany .	3	1	2	0	6	0	4
Tunisia	3	1	1	1	3	2	3
Mexico	3	0	0	3	2	12	0

GROUP 3

Austria	3	2	0	1	3	2	4
Brazil	3	1	2	0	2	1	4
Spain	3	1	1	1	2	2	3
Sweden	3	0	1	2	1	3	1

GROUP 4

Peru	3	2	1	0	7	2	5
Holland	3	1	1	1	5	3	3
Scotland	3	1	1	1	5	6	3
Iran	3	0	1	2	2	8	1

GROUP A

W. Germany 0, **Italy 0**, in Buenos Aires.

Austria 1 (Obermayer), **Holland 5** (Brandts, W. van der Kerkhof, Rensenbrink (pen), Rep (2)), in Cordoba.

Italy 1 (Rossi), **Austria 0**, in Buenos Aires.

Holland 2 (Haan, R. van der Kerkhof), **W. Germany 2** (Abramczik, D. Muller), in Cordoba.

Holland 2 (Brandts, Haan), **Italy 1** (Brandts (og)), in Buenos Aires.

Austria 3 (Vogts (og), Krankl (2)), **W. Germany 2** (Rummenigge, Holzenbein), in Cordoba.

GROUP B

Brazil 3 (Dirceu (2), Zico (pen)), **Peru 0**, in Mendoza.

Poland 0, **Argentina 2** (Kempes (2)), in Rosario.

Peru 0, **Poland 1** (Szarmach), in Mendoza.

Argentina 0, **Brazil 0**, in Rosario.

Brazil 3 (Nelinho, Roberto (2)), **Poland 1** (Lato), in Mendoza.

Argentina 6 (Kempes (2), Tarantini, Luque (2), Houseman), **Peru 0**, in Rosario.

GROUP A

	P	W	D	L	F	A	P
Holland	3	2	1	0	9	4	5
Italy	3	1	1	1	2	2	3
W. Germany	3	0	2	1	4	5	2
Austria	3	1	0	2	4	8	2

GROUP B

Argentina	3	2	1	0	8	0	5
Brazil	3	2	1	0	6	1	5
Poland	3	1	0	2	2	5	2
Peru	3	0	0	3	0	10	0

THIRD PLACE PLAY-OFF—Brazil 2 (Nelinho, Dirceu), **Italy 1** (Causio), in Buenos Aires.

FINAL—ARGENTINA 3 (Kempes (2), Bertoni), **Holland 1** (Nanninga), in Buenos Aires.

THE GREAT HAMPDEN DISASTER

Never had a Hampden Roar died with such startling suddenness. Never had a Scotland crowd been so stunned. It was the afternoon of daylight robbery, the afternoon of 20 May 1978.

Only seven minutes of the international against England remained when disaster struck. Peter Barnes, the English winger, struck a long, angled – and rather aimless – centre almost into the arms of goalkeeper Alan Rough. It should have been a gift for the Partick Thistle keeper but, hampered by Trevor Francis, he failed to clear properly, and the ball dropped in front of Steve Coppell, who couldn't believe his luck as he drove it positively into the net.

What an ending! Scotland, who had played sadly in the previous internationals against Northern Ireland and Wales, were again the heroes of their adoring supporters, playing with fire, showing more than a few glimpses of real class, and utterly outclassing their oldest enemies, who had been said to be on the way back under the guidance of manager Ron Greenwood.

But the goal that had the fans groaning was of that alarming softness which had so often before brought defeat and, in keeping with the traditions of our bad old days against England, was born of a goalkeeper's blunder. Until Rough dropped the ball at Coppell's feet, there was never a hint that England were good or dangerous enough to win.

But perhaps Scotland, who really should have been preparing for the World Cup in Argentina by playing cooler, more patient, more elegant football, were too fierce, too determined to win by power against their most bitter rivals.

Although some of their moves were exciting and fluent, there was just too much urgency about them, too much tackling that can only be described as 'crunching.'

Nevertheless, the Scots left the field with a sense of injustice – but, although beaten 1–0, they came back onto the Hampden field to wave to the crowd, who continued to flaunt their banners and shout defiant promises of what the journey to Argentina would bring.

It was a moving scene, a scene which showed just how much the fans were behind their team, but many were left wondering just how long Ally MacLeod and his players could go on believing that every disappointing rehearsal was simply further proof that the big show would come right on the day the World Cup began in South America.

Later Ally MacLeod said Scotland had outclassed England but others were of the opinion that our opponents had played with more sophistication and that the Scottish style would never do in the World Cup.

Even if for most of the game there was an avalanche of inspired pressure, no goals were scored and the crowd began to shout for the appearance of Rangers' Derek Johnstone, the man who had notched Scotland's goals in the other two home internationals but who was a substitute for this one.

Scotland had no luck, it's true. French

The goal that stopped the Hampden Roar. Steve Coppell scores for England as Scotland's Alan Rough drops the ball.

referee Konrath committed what every Scot in the crowd believed were two major errors – using the whistle too often and stopping the flow of Scotland moves and refusing to award a penalty when the ball hit the elbow of Emlyn Hughes in the area.

England saw more of the ball in the sec- ond half but they never matched the Scots in aggression.

Once again the main failure of Scotland was to put the ball in the net. There were chances alright, especially when a long cross from Willie Johnston on the left pas- sed over the head of Joe Jordan and fell right at the feet of Asa Hartford. For once, Asa's response was hopelessly inadequate, the ball bouncing away from his foot and comfortably into the hands of goalkeeper Ray Clemence.

But Hartford was the best Scot, playing incredibly well, and he received fine support from Johnston.

And even after the late substitutions of Greenhoff for Hughes, Souness and Gemmill for Masson and Rioch and Brooking for Mariner, it seemed that the team likely to take the lead, despite the frustrations near goal, was Scotland.

But then came the fatal error by Rough – and once again Scotland were left lamenting a defeat which should have been a comfortable victory.

As Ally MacLeod said: 'We did enough to win. England had one shot at goal. But Scotland did not take the chances.' Nevertheless, Scotland had lost the home series title.

The teams were:
Scotland: Rough, Kennedy, Forsyth, Burns, Donachie, Rioch, Masson, Hartford, Dalglish, Jordan, Johnston.
Subs: Gemmill, Souness, Blyth, Johnstone, Robertson.
England: Clemence, Neal, Watson, Hughes, Mills, Currie, Wilkins, Coppell, Mariner, Francis, Barnes.
Subs: Brooking, Greenhoff, Shilton, Pearson, Woodcock.
Referee: Georges Konrath, France.

Nearly there – but not quite, alas. A header from Scotland's Kenny Burns beats the English defence but the ball goes past.

THEY'RE STILL THE WIZARDS TO ME...
Fifty Years On

Season 1977–78 saw the fiftieth anniversary of what many people still consider the most legendary afternoon in the history of Scottish football – a victory more stirring, more important than winning the World Cup.

It was on the blustery afternoon of 31 March 1928, that Scotland, pitted against the auld enemy of England in the Sassenach's own capital of London, presented the most magnificent display of fluent football ever played by a British international team.

That team became the darlings of Scotland, heroes in the mould of Bruce and Wallace, the side every other international combination is compared to, the immortals ... the Wembley Wizards.

Even today old men's eyes gleam as they tell awed grandchildren of the famous 5–1 victory at Wembley ...

Of how the Scottish eleven, given no chance against the powerful English, made themselves the most magical name in soccer history in this country.

Of how the mighty midgets, wee wisps with fiery tempers and whiplash tongues, assailed opponents and each other with a Doric cacophony of yelps, bawls, complaints, snarls, advice and encouragement, and played their bigger and stronger opponents into the ground.

Of how the Wizards provided superb artistry, football as perfect as it can ever be.

Of how James, Gallacher, Morton and the rest became the wonders of all the soccer world.

Their display will never be forgotten. But time has eroded the sparkle of that occasion. There are many who denigrate the Wizards, saying we put far too much emphasis on a match of the dim past, alleging Scots in a small country of sentimentalists have really so little to boast about that we bore everyone else with never-ending tunes of glory about victories at Bannockburn and Wembley.

And some sneer at Jimmy McMullan's heroes, classing them as a modern missile expert would bowmen at Flodden, saying they couldn't live with modern international teams where the accent is on fitness, drill and power.

It's true too that the Wembley Wizards enjoyed tremendous luck and, as happens so often in these modern times, only a lucky break saved their skins.

That was admitted to me by Alex James, the king of his era, the master mechanic who made the wheels of the Wizards go round. Years afterwards he said:

'Of course, we needed luck and we got it. We got it in the writing of the critics at home. Seldom had a selection been so severely panned. We weren't given a chance – far too wee, they said. That made us mad.' His face creased into the wrinkled grin that was so endearing. 'You know what I mean, Hugh. We bristled at what you reporters wrote, as players still do I'm sure. We always believed the opposite would happen. No offence.

'But our luck was in at Wembley. It rained heavily and the pitch was treacherous. So that suited our short passing game

The daddy of them all. So many veteran fans still say. And little Alex James was indeed a Scotland hero.

and on-the-ground moves. We small chaps kept the ball down and had the English slithering all over.

'But our biggest break came in the opening minutes when the English were all over us. They should have scored when Billy Smith, the Huddersfield left-winger, slipped past our defence and hammered in a terrific shot which looked a goal all the way – until the ball hit the post.

'We breathed again and scored first. But I still don't know what would have happened to us if they had scored then. It could have been a massacre because England were a good side.

'But perhaps England were kidded by Alex Jackson.' And Alex laughed as he told tales about the debonair Alex Jackson, so confident, so full of fun. What happened, said wee James, was that just before the match the audacious Jackson was visiting his Huddersfield club-mates Smith, Wilson, Goodall and Kelly at their hotel (there were no lengthy get-togethers in those days).

'And what do you think Jackson was doing?' asked Alex. 'He was kidding the pants off his English mates, telling them how good we in the Scottish side were and how he was going to score a hat-trick.

'And he did, too! That wee talk must have worried the English.'

No-one can say now if the Wizards would have lived in present-day football. Players of today are better trained, better drilled, perhaps more intelligent, more determined to win.

But no side could have been more entertaining than the Wizards. It was a triumph of Scottish style – close co-operation between half-backs and forwards, with the ball kept on the turf, and the Wizards indulging in clockwork passing with the triangle, prettiest of all the tunes soccer can provide, tinkling for an hour and a half in the blue ranks. It was the finest Scottish forward line.

In 1928, of course, attack was still the keynote of soccer. Over the years, alas, football has become increasingly defensive, steadily denuded of attacking players. Why, in the last century, there were eight forwards and three defenders. Soon after that, the forwards were reduced to seven. Today sometimes you see only one attacker, more's the pity!

But in 1928 attack was still the name of the game and Scottish style was supreme. The greatest coach of his, and perhaps any, day knew that – Jimmy Hogan, the little man from Lancashire who preached the gospel of soccer in so many countries, the man who laid the foundations of Austrian, Hungarian and West German success. Hogan instructed in the Scottish way – the ball to be kept on the ground, the short pass, the value of positional play, the player always looking for and moving into the open space, all five forwards to stay up the field.

Not only the Wizards were the idols of the fans. During the late twenties Scotland had many notable players and here are the men who played for the Scottish League against the English League at Birmingham in Nov, 1928 – L to R (back row) – McNab (Dundee), Battles (Hearts), Gray (Rangers), J.Thomson (Celtic), Blair (Clyde), McDonald (Rangers), Bennie (Hearts). Front row – Archibald (Rangers), A Thomson (Celtic), McGrory (Celtic), McStay (Celtic), McAlpine (Queen's Park), Morton (Rangers).

Is this not the 'total' football of the Dutch and Germans and Brazilians of today?

Hogan and the Wizards preached finesse over force. Maybe play is more robust today, but for sheer entertainment no international team, not even the Hungarians or Brazilians, have beaten the Wembley Wizards.

So let's praise them, admire them, remember them. In these days when football is often violent and negative, when games are so often sterile, sometimes nasty, the play and manner of the Wizards – and, don't forget, of the English, who refused to resort to the niggling tactics employed by losing sides today – made football a proud game.

We will never see the likes of the Wizards again. Football tends to mirror its age and we are now in an age of violence. The artistry of James and Co just wouldn't be tolerated. We all know what happened when Celtic played Racing of Buenos Aires in the World Cup Championship, when Manchester United met Estudiantes in the same title chase. The British players were ruthlessly spat on, hacked, punched, bloodied. There's too much jungle law in football now, so we will never have a team of Wizards.

But their memory – the memory of pure, clean, enjoyable football, football as it should be played – will never die. And that's why I refuse to listen to anyone who denigrates Scotland's most tasteful, dexterous, graceful, distinctive, and illustrious international eleven.

AYE, IT'S A HARD GAME FOOTBALL...

Old-timers shake their heads and say: 'Ach, fitba's no' whit it was. It's no' nearly as hard nooadays.'

Oh, isn't it?

Football, in fact, is probably tougher than it ever was. Rewards are higher, the cost of failure dearer. Players are better trained, fitter, more determined.

It's true the lads today aren't kitted out in those famous Manfield Hotspur football boots whose toes could do so much damage.

But football is as tough as ever – often a hard, sore game.

You don't think so?

Just have a look at these pictures, then, and see if you don't change your mind. . . .

'Ouch, that was sore,' gasps Hibs centre-half George Stewart as two desperate Partick Thistle attackers bump him out of the way in a bid to get to the ball.

'And so was that,' cries Celtic's Joe Craig as he goes to earth with a bang.

Above:
'Keep the head, boys,' demands Rangers' Alex Miller as tempers boil over during a match with Motherwell.

Right:
They all go bump together ... it's a rear-end collision during a Partick Thistle v Dumbarton match.

Opposite above:
'Gosh, they don't half make it tough training at Firhill' – that's the view of Partick Thistle's famous goalkeepers, Alan Rough and Billy Thomson, kept going during a practice spin.

Opposite below:
'That's enough, mate, jolly well push off,' snorts Dumbarton goalkeeper Lawrie Williams after an incident involving Doug Somner of Partick Thistle.

Who said footballers led the soft life? Not these Rangers stars, going all out at training.

'Help, I'm sinking' says Derek Johnstone of Rangers, vanquished by Ayr United defenders.

GORDON'S 'EXTRA' SPECIAL WINNER

It was Gordon Smith's finest moment – a moment Rangers' £65 000 buy from Kilmarnock will never forget. It was the moment last-gasp Gordon scored an extra special winner.

Only two minutes of the Old Firm League Cup Final at Hampden on 18 March 1978 remained. Many of the fans had departed for they were all sure that the match, which had gone to extra time, would end in a draw.

Rangers appeared to have lost their chance. Until Smith struck.

Over came a cross from substitute Alex Miller. Up went Celtic goalkeeper Peter Latchford, who had played impeccably, and Rangers' little Alex MacDonald. There was a clash. For once Latchford failed to clear. And the ball broke to the elegant Smith, who dived to head into the net.

Rangers had won the League Cup.

And they won it because of Smith and David Cooper, another Ranger playing in his first final, to set a record in winning the

Two great acquisitions by Rangers – Davie Cooper from Clydebank and Gordon Smith from Kilmarnock.

Let-off for Rangers. Ronnie Glavin has a chance but blasts the ball against the post.

trophy for the ninth time (compared with Celtic's eight) and start their bid for the grand slam of League Cup, Scottish Cup and Premier League. For it was Cooper, once with Clydebank, who scored the first Rangers goal.

Alas, it was anything but a classic final. But the goals were dramatic and Celtic rose from the ashes of a disappointing season to come close to winning the League Cup, the only major prize that was available to them in March, 1978.

Mistakes brought drama if not distinction to the Final and it was Celtic's misfortune that two of the three errors were made by their players.

The first sensation for the crowd of 60 168 who watched the Final, postponed until the spring because of bad weather earlier in the season, came when Stewart Kennedy made a magnificent save from Celtic's Roy Aitken.

pointment in the 38th minute when they got the goal they deserved. It came because of an error by Ronnie Glavin of Celtic who made the mistake of trying to shepherd the ball out of play. In nipped Smith, the thoroughbred, to clip the ball from his opponent's toes, cross and dance away happily as he saw David Cooper slam a goal past the helpless Latchford.

It was a disappointing final, a game lacking the excitement of Old Firm encounters and riddled with fouls. Five players were booked – Edvaldsson, Lynch and Doyle of Celtic and MacDonald and McLean of Rangers – and the referee had to speak to several others.

The second half was hardly an epic. As time rolled on, Celtic pressed but lacked the power and skill to pierce the Rangers defence. Then, looking down and out, Celtic saw the miracle happen. With only five minutes of normal time left, Stewart Kennedy in the Rangers goal boobed.

Out on the right, young Alan Sneddon, the defender who had taken over from the injured Danny McGrain and who had played with a veteran's assurance in his first big game, crossed. Kennedy, arms flailing, didn't get to the ball. And there was Jo Edvaldsson, Celtic's versatile Icelander, meeting the ball at the far post and crashing in a header off the underside of the bar.

That goal sparked off the most exciting football of the whole match. Extra time provided the most intriguing play and Celtic looked like winning, with a shot being cleared off the Rangers line and Rangers fans whistling with relief as other tries went past.

Celtic's luck was out, though. Latchford erred – and so Rangers won because of their late goal. It was fitting that Smith scored the winner for he was the best attacker on the field, his speedy runs revealing chinks in the Celtic defence.

Yet Celtic were unlucky, especially in extra time when they played the crisper, smoother football. Rangers, who had

Then there was fury in the blue ranks in the 24th minute. A foray by skipper John Greig ... his cross breaking to Derek Johnstone ... the ball in the net from the big attacker ... and Rangers going wild with delight.

Joy turned to anger when referee David Syme ruled that Greig, who had run over the by-line, was offside and chalked off the goal. So there were plenty of complaints from the Rangers players.

However, Rangers forgot their disap-

brought back Johnny Hamilton in midfield, lacked the organization they were so proud of when Bobby Russell, out because of injury, was in the side.

After Rangers took the lead, they went, surprisingly, on defence and when Celtic grabbed the equaliser it seemed as though they could win.

In the tense, tight match it was obvious that only mistakes would bring results.

Fear was the name of the game in a shoddy showpiece of a final, with precious little good football, too much niggling, and few flashes of skill.

Thank goodness for Smith, one of the few players at Hampden who brought distinction and a touch of real Scottish style to a drab occasion.

Again Celtic worried about the lack of a smile from Dame Fortune in the League Cup Final. Just by appearing they made history in the form of a world record for a fourteenth successive League Cup Final. But they had won only one of their last seven matches in the climax of this competition. And in March, 1978, they lost again.

One nice touch about a forgettable final was that Bobby Russell, who missed the match because of a virus, got a winners medal after all.

Minutes after the whistle, Sandy Jardine presented his badge to Bobby in the dressing room. It was his first medal and as Bobby said: 'I was overwhelmed by Sandy's generosity.'

Most neutrals were glad the Old Firm weren't paired in the season's remaining glamour game, the Scottish Cup Final. It seems that almost unbearable tension surrounds the Rangers – Celtic clashes and the Premier League, with the four club battles every season, and the continued domination

What a goal – by Davie Cooper of Rangers. He gives goalkeeper Peter Latchford of Celtic no chance.

It's all over. Rangers have won the cup – and it's a field day for the photographers.

of the domestic scene by Glasgow's big Two has intensified these pressures.

The teams in the League Cup Final were:
Celtic: Latchford, Sneddon, Lynch, Munro, MacDonald, Dowie, Glavin, Edvaldsson, McCluskey, Aitken, Burns. Wilson and Doyle came on for Lynch and Glavin.

Rangers: Kennedy, Jardine, Greig, Forsyth, Jackson, MacDonald, McLean, Hamilton, Johnstone, Smith, Cooper. Parlane and Miller came on for Hamilton and Cooper.

Referee: D. Syme, Glasgow.

NIGHTS OF GLORY

Two matches which will never be forgotten were played in season 1977–78; two matches which put Scotland on the way to the World Cup Finals in the Argentine; two matches which made the players once again the darlings of the fantastic Scottish football fans.

They were the games against Czechoslovakia and Wales in the qualifying section of the World Cup.

They were the games which will be talked about as long as football is played.

Dream night at Hampden

The match was long over, but still the yellow standards fluttered, still the chant of 'Oh, Flo'er o' Scotland' resounded over Hampden and still the 85 000 fans who had cheered Scotland to an epic World Cup qualifying victory on that wonderful night of Wednesday, 21 September 1977, wouldn't leave the stadium.

They wanted to salute the men who had beaten Czechoslovakia 3–1 in a lap of honour.

But manager Ally MacLeod said, rightly: 'This was a great victory – but it wasn't a night for a lap of honour. We'll do that when we qualify for the World Cup Finals.'

So the fans at last disappeared into the autumn night, singing happily, convinced Scotland were Argentina-bound after such a wonderful display.

Always on top – that's striker Joe Jordan.

41

Nothing could dampen Scottish delight for Scotland had scored a victory to be cherished, a victory which put Ally MacLeod's players back on the football map.

With the tango tunes of the Argentine ringing in their ears, the valiant men in blue played modern but powerful football, laced, however, with golden old-fashioned touches which had once made us supreme in soccer.

Every Scot played his part. The Czechs were the team Scotland had to beat and they played well enough – but only as well as the commanding Scots allowed them to play.

After only 18 minutes, Hampden went wild as Scotland scored the opening goal, the goal which mattered so much. And what a spectacular effort it was!

It came from the much-criticized Joe Jordan, so brave but so often sneered at because he didn't get the goals his critics believed he should score. But Jordan was playing with all his lion-hearted prowess, allying great skill to strength.

Over came an accurate corner from winger Willie Johnston and Hampden became a tartan carnival as Jordan headed past goalkeeper Pavol Michalik.

Some breathed a sigh of relief that at last the keeper had proved he was only human. Before that, in an atmosphere that made the scalp tingle, the coolest man on that tense pitch had been Michalik.

How the Scots groaned as the splendid new Czech keeper dived in just before Kenny Dalglish to stop a hot raid. How they sighed as twice the daring man in the sweater brilliantly saved fierce shots from Dalglish and Don Masson.

It was a nail-biting occasion as Michalik gave his colleagues confidence and the Czechs began to reveal clever touches. But that Jordan goal cheered up the fans – for a minute or two.

Then gloom set in again. For a depressing spell Scotland faltered. They lost their rhythm and the Czechs darted in. That was when the Scotland defence showed how

Hot action, with Kenny Dalglish in the thick of it, during the hectic World Cup qualifying match between Wales and Scotland at Anfield.

good they were. They broke up the brisk Czech attacks.

And Scotland bloomed again.

In 35 minutes another Johnston-Jordan link-up brought a second goal. Scotland had taken the game in hand again. The gale of cheers broke out once more. Masson, Rioch and Hartford seized a firm grip. Attacks flowed freely and fluently and at last the Czechs were anxiously packing their penalty area. Then Johnston put the ball over from the left. Jordan rose, a king of the air. He was fouled, but he pressed on. The keeper collided with him, the ball broke, and Hampden was a shrieking yell of tartan delight as Asa Hartford was on the spot to slot the ball into the net for Scotland's No 2.

The Czechs sagged for the Scots were massively on top, tackling tigerishly, with Bruce Rioch playing a captain's part, but also revealing slick, sometimes silken, skill.

In 54 minutes, the Scots added a third, wonderful goal. A corner was partially cleared. And there was Sandy Jardine lying handy outside the penalty area to nod the ball back into the battle zone. Kenny Dalglish, goal-snatcher supreme, flicked his head venomously to speed the ball past Michalik.

The only moment of sorrow for Scotland on a memorable night was when they seemed to falter near the end and lost concentration. That was when winger Gajdusek was allowed to run on and shoot. Goalkeeper Alan Rough, for once, was caught and the ball slipped into the net at the post.

It didn't matter. Scotland had shown they had the skill, and guts and confidence to win their way to the World Cup Finals. Scotland were great again.

Ken Dalglish, toast of the Liverpool Kop, shows his skill – but this time he's playing for Scotland against Wales.

The Czechs never looked as though they were champions of Europe. They never really got a chance to, so good were Scotland.

Certainly Czech skipper Pollak showed true Continental class – but the Czechs, frankly, never stood a chance against the combined talents of a proud Scottish team and the tremendous vocal support of the greatest fans in the world.

How good are the Scottish fans? Skipper Bruce Rioch summed it up like this: 'They're just the best. I've never known a noise like that.

'We couldn't hear each other shouting if we were more than five yards apart. The noise was unbelievable.'

For Scotland and Czechoslovakia, it was a repeat performance. Four years before Scotland had defeated the Czechs to go through to the World Cup Finals in West Germany.

The teams:

Scotland: Rough, Jardine, McGrain, Forsyth, McQueen, Rioch, Masson, Dalglish, Jordan, Hartford, Johnston. Subs: Stewart, Macari, Johnstone, Gemmill, Harper.

Czechoslovakia: Michalik, Paurik, Capkovic, Dvorak, Geogh, Dobia, Gajdusek, Moder, Pollak, Masny, Nehoda. Subs: Knapp, Kozak, Gallisa, Vojacek, Zlamal.

Referee: Francois Rion, Belgium.

A big hand for Scotland

A hand played a big part in the tartan dream coming true on a sensational night in Liverpool on Wednesday 12 October 1977.

But whose hand was it?

Welshmen to this day say it was that of Scotland's Joe Jordan. Scots, of course, aver it was that of Wales's Davy Jones.

It doesn't matter now because French referee Robert Wurtz, right on the spot, had no doubt, and even though television shots

Little Lou Macari, the buzz-bomb of Scotland.

seemed to prove it was Jordan's hand that was up in the air, the referee awarded Scotland a penalty – which really goes to prove that all the television shows isn't necessarily true, that the camera can lie, and that, if you want to know what actually goes on in soccer, you've got to attend the matches and not watch them from the comfort of your armchair.

What a night it was at Liverpool's Anfield. The match between Wales and Scotland was played there because Wales, the home country, couldn't find a ground capable of safely holding the big crowd, and felt that Anfield was the next best thing to a Welsh ground.

And what a mistake that was! For more than 30 000 Scots – Ally's Tartan Army – gained precious tickets by hook or by crook and made the vital qualifying match another home game for Scotland.

Indeed, there seemed to be hardly a Welshman in sight on another never-to-be-forgotten Scotland international night.

It wasn't easy for Scotland, though. Indeed, never were a Scotland team more relieved to win a game. Never did the side come back so magnificently after being right out of the picture.

It was a tragedy for Davy Jones, the young reserve who had been brought into the weakened Welsh side, that brought Scotland victory.

Only 12 minutes to go. Scotland struggling. At last, space found on the left. A throw-in from Willie Johnston – long and menacing. Up went heads – and a hand. To the consternation of the Welsh and the delight of the Scots, referee Wurtz at once awarded a penalty.

Was it Jones's hand? Or Jordan's? Or was Jordan pushed before the ball came over? We'll never know. The referee was in no doubt. And few Welshmen – significantly – protested.

Scotland skipper Don Masson didn't care. He assumed the responsibility of taking one of the most vital penalties in our football history. Coolly, dispassionately, he stroked the ball past goalkeeper Dai Davies.

And from that moment on the Scots knew they were already on the plane to the World Cup Finals in the Argentine. As the new anthem, 'Oh, Flo'er o' Scotland' reverberated from the packed terracings into the sombre Liverpool sky, there was even better to come.

Three minutes from time – and there arrived a magnificent goal, a goal worthy of a World Cup Final! And it was fitting that Kenny Dalglish, former Celt who was the new hero of Liverpool's Kop, scored it.

Martin Buchan, who had come on for the injured Sandy Jardine, sent over a fine cross from the right and Dalglish soared gleefully to rocket the ball with his head into the net.

That was the end for the brave Welsh – and the start of a new World Cup era for the Scots.

Both Scottish goals came from high balls – a shy from the left and a cross from the right. But this mode of attack, the attack the Scottish team know so well, was left until the end of the match.

Despite the celebrations, despite the jubilation, everyone realized the Scots didn't look like World Cup contenders and were blue ghosts of the splendid side who had thrashed the Czechs not so long before.

What went wrong? Too much tension, too much worry about the game? Perhaps.

Yet Scotland should have had the game wrapped up after 15 minutes. At the start, they stormed into a Welsh side that appeared dumbfounded at the spectacle on the terracings – a wonderland of Scottish ferocity and gaiety, a tartan nightmare for the Welsh.

But they were tormented by tension. Chances came and went. Kenny Dalglish unaccountably missed a glorious chance after a shocking Welsh defensive blunder. Through on his own, Dalglish slipped as Dai Davies challenged him. He appealed for a penalty but the referee waved play on. It should have been a certain goal.

Wales took heart. They began to command the middle, the middle in which Scotland believed they had the pick of Europe. But Yorath, Mahoney and Flynn were much stronger and more flexible than Don Masson and company, who were missing the injured Bruce Rioch. And the Scottish attack was stifled.

Desperation set in. There was no adventure on the wings. Our midfield stuttered and stumbled, and – worse – the Scottish defence appeared baffled and bewildered when John Toshack and Mike Thomas, only a Wrexham reserve, took the game boldly to the Scots.

Indeed, Alan Rough had to make one of the greatest saves of his career when he tipped over the bar a beautifully-placed lob by Toshack, the ball bouncing on the bar before going over.

The anxiety of Scotland was shown when Willie Donachie was booked for a foul on Mahoney and, as this was his second caution in the World Cup qualifying series, he missed the first Scotland game in the Argentine.

Suddenly, however, Scotland pulled themselves together. When the fans, worried and sick, became silent at last, believing a goal-less draw was inevitable, that was when the boys in blue found new courage, new strength and regained their poise.

The closing minutes were glorious – and that was what mattered.

Scotland were on the road to Argentina.

The teams:
Scotland: Rough, Jardine, Donachie, Forsyth, McQueen, Masson, Dalglish, Hartford, Jordan, Macari, Johnston. Buchan came on for Jardine.
Wales: Davies, R. Thomas, D. Jones, Phillips, J. Jones, Mahoney, Yorath, Flynn, Sayer, Toshack, M. Thomas.
Referee: Robert Wurtz, France.

That's the way to do it, Don. And Masson scores a vital penalty for Scotland against Wales.

The Scottish supporters left Anfield confused and angry, however. They were robbed of the chance of saluting their World Cup heroes because the Liverpool police banned a lap of honour.

Jubilant fans remained on the terracings long after the final whistle, chanting for the players to come out. But the Liverpool police decided the Scots should stay in the dressing room. Nevertheless, celebrations went on long into the night.

Scotland had once again fought their way to the finals of the World Cup – and what made it all the sweeter for the Scots was that their team were the only British representatives in the Argentine.

BILLY STEEL - the Greatest of them all

Who was the greatest Scottish footballer?

That's one of the surest ways I know of starting an argument. For everyone has his own favourite and don't think you can change an opinion because there is no-one more dogmatic than the football fan.

And the range is wide. Some favour Gordon Smith, that cavalier of the wing. Others believe that Alan Morton, the wee blue devil, was easily the most accomplished player this country produced. Denis Law, prince of attackers, has his supporters. So has Jim Baxter, so suave, football poetry in motion. And what about big George Young, defender superb? And John Thomson, that magnificent but tragic goalkeeper? And Hughie Gallacher, the moody genius? Or Jimmy McGrory, the goal-scoring machine? Or a dozen more.

It's a long list, for Scotland, more than any other country, has been blessed with wonderful players – forwards, defenders, half-backs, powerful warriors, sophisticated artists.

It is, however, of inside-forwards that the Scottish troubadours sing and the heroic tales are told. And the reason for this lies in the Scot's respect for craftsmanship. The inside-forward is the engineer of the team. While there is always the flamboyant character whose dearest dream is to score the winning goal for Scotland at Hampden, the majority of football enthusiasts in this country would rather be inside-forwards.

That's the position I favoured but, alas, none of the genius of the Scottish greats was

Billy Steel as he was in his heyday with Dundee – the best inside-forward of them all.

seen in my play and my career was brief and undistinguished and the only cheer I ever received was when I informed my club committee that I was packing up the game.

My shortcomings as a player, however, did not prevent me from becoming a keen student of the art of inside-forward play, in which position Scotland produced one master after another. They didn't all play alike and there appeared to be a world of diffe

48

Kenny Dalglish about to beat a Dutch defender.

Joe Jordan gives Holland's defence a hard time.

Hot action in the Scotland –
Ireland international.

Top right: Asa Hartford
starts a cute move at Hampden in the Scotland – England match.

Right: New Scotland star
Stuart Kennedy goes into
the attack against England.

Far right: Defender Willie
Donachie clearing an Eng-
land attack at Hampden.

Scotland captain Bruce
Rioch in a clash in the match
with Ireland

Determined Jo Edvaldsson
of Celtic wins the ball in the
League Cup Final.

Opposite top left: Kenny
Burns of Scotland and Nottingham Forest – the player
of the year south of the border.

Opposite top right: Aberdeen goalkeeper Bobby
Clark.

Left: A tough tussle in the
Celtic – Rangers League Cup
Final.

Rangers' elegant stars –
Bobby Russell and Gordon
Smith.

Above left: Sandy Jardine of Rangers.

Above right: Derek Johnstone of Rangers and John McMaster of Aberdeen.

Left: Rangers' Davie Cooper trying to find a way past Aberdeen defenders in the Scottish Cup Final.

Opposite top left: Flying high is Scotland's Gordon McQueen playing at Ibrox in the John Greig testimonial match.

Opposite top right: It's Scotland's favourite player – little Archie Gemmill of Nottingham Forest.

Right: Joe Jordan and Tom Forsyth go for the ball in the John Greig testimonial.

Aberdeen mount a hot attack against Partick Thistle.

Hibs' Arthur Duncan finds a way past Celtic's Alan Stockton and Roy Aitken.

ence between the silky play of, say, Jimmy Mason and the robust approach of Bob McPhail.

Yet at the heart of their play was the same beat. They were all masters of design. Even those of baroque genius, even those whose principal asset was a spectacular burst through a bewildered defence, were essentially builders. Like a Clydeside engineer, they pinned their faith on stout construction, a smooth movement, a distinctive touch and true Scottish craft. They were all painstaking in their efforts to make their teams flow. They knew they were the mainsprings, the men whose job was to construct the pads from which the missiles flew.

So my choice of the greatest Scottish player must be an inside-forward – or midfield man, in the modern jargon.

But which? For me, it is an agonizing decision. For years I was convinced that the crown must go to Alex James, that small, bullet-headed chatterbox who always wore long flapping pants that were the delight of the cartoonists, the centre parting that was the trademark of so many Scottish sporting heroes of the twenties and thirties, and buttoned sleeves.

James worked miracles of sleight-of-foot. He had uncanny anticipation. His passing was incredibly accurate.

I was biased of course. I was a friend and I knew just how much kindliness abounded in his small frame and I agreed with George Allison, former manager of James's Arsenal, when he declared that 'Alex James was the greatest exponent of all the arts and crafts known to Association football.'

But that was before football changed its style. And the man most deserving of a stained-glass window is the player who would have been supreme in all styles of soccer.

Certainly James would have stood out in any era. But I now consider that there is another inside-forward more deserving of the title because, I believe, this man, thanks to his physique and his burning desire to win, would have been more successful in present-day football than wee Alex.

Billy Steel.

Steel who had springs for muscles. Steel who had a choirboy's face that masked a devouring, often ruthless, determination to achieve football perfection. Steel who had a caustic tongue that frequently angered team-mates more bitterly than opponents. Steel who had a style and ability that, today, would have had the wealthy clubs of Europe bidding frantically for his transfer. Steel who belonged to the elite corps of international players, the global greats like Beckenbauer, Cruyff, Pele, Di Stefano, Puskas, Kopa, Seeler, Rivera.

Steel was ageless and classless and would have been a success with Inter Milan or Bayern Munich, Manchester United or Rangers, Penarol or Santos.

His secret was the same as Denis Law's – an agile brain, a puma's pounce and extraordinary gymnastic ability which put him invariably a move ahead of his colleagues. There was nothing svelte about Steel. He exuded vitality; he had the killer instinct of a Benny Lynch; he was the type of aggressive attacker who was so keen to win he would have sworn at his best friend if he felt that man hadn't been pulling his weight. It's true that Steel flashed across the football firmament like a meteor – transient but brilliant. Few players made such an impression on the game by sheer genius. And he made headline news almost from the moment he first kicked a ball.

In 1937 Steel, who had been born in Denny, was capped as a schoolboy for Scotland, with George Young in the same team.

In 1939 scores of scouts were after him. He went to Leicester City but, as he was under-age, the English club couldn't hold him and in August of that year he played his first game as a senior for St Mirren against Rangers at Ibrox. Again he was too young to sign as a professional.

Billy Steel pictured on a recent visit home to Scotland. He's still a football enthusiast.

In 1940 on his seventeenth birthday, he signed his first professional contract with Morton.

In 1946 he was demobbed from the army and re-joined Morton.

In 1947 he played his first international match against England at Wembley and, in May, he was outstanding in the Great Britain team that beat the Rest of Europe at Hampden – and this was real fame for Steel, for the selectors passed over inside-forwards of the calibre of Raich Carter, Peter Doherty,

Jimmy Hagan, Len Shackleton and Stan Mortensen in the Morton man's favour.

In June 1947 he was transferred to Derby County for a £15 500 fee after a sensational Continental tour with Scotland.

From 1947 to 1950 Steel reached the peak of his career, became an automatic choice for Scotland and was nicknamed the Blond Bombshell.

In 1950 he was transferred to Dundee for £23 000 after an argument with Derby about his desire to live in Glasgow. He had refused re-signing offers for five months.

From 1950 to 1953 Dundee had great years, thanks largely to the genius of Steel.

50

whose presence on the field attracted huge crowds. Dundee won the League Cup twice and reached the final of the 1952 Scottish Cup.

In 1953 the sensation of the season was provided when Dundee dropped Steel and he remained a spectator for five weeks.

In 1954 Steel emigrated to the United States, where he is now a businessman.

At Dundee Steel revolutionized the team, and their style, which was to become famous, was fashioned round him. Steel brought adventure back to Scottish football. His speed off the mark, his fiery dash, his thundering shot, his facility for appearing in the open space – these were the wonderful qualities which make him, in the opinion of many others apart from myself, The Very Best Scottish Footballer.

Steel had a fetish about fitness. I saw him in his great days at training giving displays of handsprings and somersaults which would have made him a hit in a circus – an example of the agility that made him such a notable footballer. He could walk the breadth of a football pitch on his hands.

And could he shoot! Perhaps his finest goal was scored against the Rest of Europe at Hampden. It was a tremendous shot from 25 yards which beat goalkeeper Da Rui, the Frenchman who was screaming 'Regardez Steel' to no avail. Steel had collected the ball almost on the half-way line, ran on and then unleashed that fantastic shot which blurred past the keeper.

That was Steel – tremendous player, great character, controversial, caustic in the tradition of Patsy Gallacher, Tommy McInally and those few others whose personalities were as dominating as their soccer brilliance.

He played thirty-four times for Scotland, that pocket Hercules who was cocky, pugnacious and highly intelligent and who was known to tell his colleagues that they were 'a bunch of mugs'.

Billy liked to order people about and when he and George Young were in the same

Is he the new Billy Steel? Yes, it's Kenny Dalglish, now with Liverpool and the hero of the Kop, but seen here as thousands of Parkhead fans remember him – the captain of Celtic.

international side Scotland always had two captains. Steely was skipper up front and Corky Young bossed the defence. It worked for both were leaders in their own fashion.

So it's Steel for me as the best Scottish footballer.

Maybe you've other ideas. Good. But you won't change my opinion – any more than I'll change yours!

51

THE HONOURS GRADUATES – from Ibrox and Parkhead

The influence of the Old Firm of Rangers and Celtic on Scottish football was never more significant than in January 1978, when the draw for the third round of the Scottish Cup was made. For no fewer than eleven of the managers of the clubs involved were former players for Glasgow's Big Two.

The fact that Parkhead and Ibrox are the top schools for football managers was proved by the roll call of managers for the cup ties, which included: Celtic v Dundee, Partick Thistle v Cowdenbeath, St Mirren v Kilmarnock, Berwick Rangers v Rangers, Arbroath v Motherwell, Hamilton Academicals v Dundee United, Aberdeen v Ayr United, Queen of the South v Montrose, Alloa v Dumbarton, Albion Rovers v Morton.

Seven of the managers were former Celts – Jock Stein (Celtic), Billy McNeill (Aberdeen), Bertie Auld (Partick Thistle), Tommy Gemmell (Dundee), Benny Rooney (Morton), Mike Jackson (Queen of the South), Eric Smith (Hamilton Acas).

Four had come through the ranks at Ibrox – Alex Ferguson (St Mirren), Roger Hynd (Motherwell), Davie Wilson (Dumbarton), Dave Smith (Berwick Rangers.)

The Old Firm have already produced most of Scotland's football managers. Who will be the next from Rangers and Celtic to step into a boss's chair?

John Greig of Rangers, pictured here at an Ibrox gala evening, with famous old timers behind him.

52

The Old Firm have dominated Scottish football for a century on the field. Now it looks as though their ex-players will form an elite corps of managers.

What is the secret of the Old Firm?

It is alleged that Rangers and Celtic are usually the winners on the pitch because of their fame and their wealth – that practically every promising player in Scotland wants to play for one or other of them, that they can offer better terms to the lads that they seek, that Old Firm stars don't have to be transferred to England because their futures are assured.

I feel that the Old Firm now produces managers galore because, despite all the sneers which arise through envy of the Glasgow giants, these clubs have something no others possess.

For instance, Rangers are much more than a football team. They are a public school, a university, a business college, a finishing school for life. They are as tradition-conscious as Eton or a crack regiment. The ghosts and reputations of the magnificent men of the past haunt Ibrox and still mould the youngsters.

The Ibrox way of life was imposed by manager Bill Struth, the image of the successful Glasgow businessman. Well proportioned, impeccably dressed, he insisted that nothing but the best was good enough for any Rangers player. Nothing was too small to be ignored. Players' collars had to be turned down and exactly one inch of black had to be shown above the red band of the stocking.

There still is an Ibrox mystique, a compound of strengths and one or two weaknesses, fads and fancies, superstitions and hoodoos. But the quality that overrides everything else is club spirit, and pride in the club. That's why Rangers players, geared to success and allowed into the secret of what

Willie Miller and Billy McNeill before the Cup Final.

makes success, have a better chance than most of becoming successful managers.

Celtic, too, are more than a club. They are also traditionalists, insist on the highest standards of conduct and discipline, and make team spirit supreme.

And they have Jock Stein, man of miracles. Any players with ambition to become bosses themselves who have been under the guidance of the Celtic manager must have a start over most other aspirants.

There are, of course, other reasons why former Old Firm stars enter managership. Says Davie Smith of Berwick: 'If you've played for Celtic or Rangers, many doors which otherwise might be kept closed to you are opened. You've a better chance than a similar man who has learned his football with one of the smaller clubs.'

Could be. And that might appear to be the case for Billy McNeill and Tommy Gemmell who walked into big jobs as managers of Aberdeen and Dundee respectively with virtually no experience as bosses or coaches.

The former Celtic captain had two months' apprenticeship with Clyde, but beat highly experienced candidates for the Pittodrie job. Gemmell walked straight from the Dens Park dressing room to the manager's chair. Nevertheless, both have done extremely well since they became managers.

As Billy McNeill points out: 'Playing for the Old Firm makes it easier to become known and to keep your name in the public eye.'

But there's much more to it than that. Adds McNeill: 'One important feature is that the Old Firm attitude is so much more demanding than it is elsewhere. You are expected to win every week. And this develops an appetite for winning which certainly doesn't switch off when you stop playing.'

And the new managers all agree that they have learned from great Old Firm bosses.

Alex Ferguson, St Mirren and Aberdeen, says: 'I thought Scot Symon (now with Partick Thistle) was the perfect model for any young manager in his complete grasp of all the different sides of the job, from administrative work right through to the team.'

And Davie Wilson considers that the most important quality the Old Firm instil into their players is the ability to live with pressure.

Certainly coolness under fire is a common quality among the big band of bosses bred by Celtic and Rangers. Another is their driving ambition, their determination to be successful – mottoes which hang over Ibrox and Parkhead in headline type.

One of these days managers will probably need a degree before they get a job – and the most coveted will be the honours degrees from the soccer universities of Ibrox and Parkhead.

Former Celtic star Harry Hood, whose other clubs have included Clyde, Motherwell and Queen of the South, would obviously turn into a first-class manager.

ABUNE THEM A'...

Scottish football was flying high last season, with our great team in blue the only British country to qualify for the World Cup.

There was plenty of action too on the Scottish grounds – as these dramatic pictures from the big games show.

High into the air soars Celtic centre-half Roddie MacDonald as he joins in an attack on the Rangers goal in an Old Firm battle.

A battle in the air is won by Ayr United's Rikky
Fleming as Derek Johnstone of Rangers tries to
beat the defenders.

Acrobatic goalkeeper Hugh Sproat of Ayr makes
an unusual and spectacular save.

58

Come on, ref, have a heart! — that's the appeal made by Hibernian goalkeeper Mike MacDonald. Hard-hearted referee John Paterson turns a deaf ear. He says it's a penalty — and that's that.

What a goal! Celtic goalkeeper Peter Latchford hasn't a chance with this one, as Rangers' Gordon Smith hammers the ball past him.

Following pages:
A goal to remember — and Stewart Rennie of Motherwell has no chance with this flashing shot from Alex MacDonald of Rangers.

61

One of Scottish football's best and steadiest
defenders, Joe Wark of Motherwell, clears from
Joe Craig of Celtic.

Hey, keep your hands off me! Celtic's Johnny
Doyle and Dundee United's Frank Kopel seem to
be doing a waltz as they tangle.

Rangers' wee wizard Tom McLean in action
against Brian Rodman and Rikky Fleming, of Ayr
United.

MY SOCCER INDIAN SUMMER
by Alex Rae of Forfar Athletic

My indian summer as a soccer player began in one of the unlikeliest places of all – Meadowbank Stadium in Edinburgh.

It was there that little Forfar Athletic played their first League Cup tie of last season. The first game in a run that saw one of Scotland's most unfashionable clubs come so close to making history. And I was proud to be part of that famous League Cup run, particularly as it came when I thought my career was finished.

When Cowdenbeath released me at the end of the previous season, I really thought my playing career was over. I had one offer in the next few weeks, from Nairn County in the Highland League.

I would probably have taken it but for the fact that no coaching was involved and I didn't fancy moving my family up north on what was likely to be a short-term agreement.

It was while I was attending the SFA coaching course at Inverclyde House, Largs, that I crossed paths with Forfar player-manager Archie Knox.

He watched me play in a bounce game during the course and must have felt that I still had something to offer and that is how I came to be fixed up at Station Park ... how I set off on a road that was to make me as happy as I was when I actually won the League Cup as skipper of Partick Thistle in season 1971–72.

Alex Rae of Forfar Athletic, formerly captain of Partick Thistle.

There was nothing remarkable in the way it started at Meadowbank, a 2–2 draw and a 2–0 win for us in the second leg at Station Park.

It was after that that the whole soccer world started to sit up and take notice of a club whose sole ambition in the past always appeared to be to finish second to last in the Scottish League.

Our next tie paired us with Ayr United and we created a minor stir by losing only 2–1 at Somerset Park in the first leg.

We felt we had a chance of beating the Premier League side in the return game at Station Park but our hopes were dimmed when they went ahead.

But, even though we were down 3–1 on aggregate, we managed to get our game together after a shaky start to the second half.

And suddenly everything fell into place for us. In the space of ten minutes late in the game Forfar found a brave new image.

I started it with a goal, Kenny Payne got another to make it 3–3 on aggregate and finally little Henry Hall scored the clincher. We were in the next round.

However, there was a sense of anti-climax when we heard the quarter-final draw. It was the last one we wanted – Queen of the South, at Palmerston in the first leg.

It wasn't likely to boost the club's bank balance and there was a very good chance that we would lose. After all, Queens had planted six goals in the back of the Dundee net at Palmerston in the previous round.

But what a night it was to prove for the club and for myself. After losing an early goal I equalised from a penalty.

Two more goals by Queens, however, and our cup run seemed to be about to grind to a halt. Those six goals they had hit against Dundee were fresh in our minds.

But again we just kept plugging away until we were able to stage a recovery. And suddenly I hit two more goals to give us a 3–3 draw.

I'll never forget the scenes after that Dumfries game. Our dressing-room was full of players, officials, fans, the lot. I think it was the happiest scene I had ever witnessed at any football ground.

However, we still had to beat them to achieve the impossible dream, a place in the semi-final.

I think it was then that the pressure began to hit us . . . suddenly we realized how close we were to a little bit of soccer history.

There was a lot of tension in the dressing-room before the second leg and it wasn't helped when we heard that the game would be delayed because of traffic chaos around the town. Imagine that! Traffic jams in Forfar for a football match!

But it was true and, in fact, Queens were caught up in it. It was 7.15 before they arrived and the match kicked off twenty minutes late with the ground packed.

This was the moment of truth and we knew it. It told in our play for a time but the whole place went crazy when Billy Gavin scored after twenty minutes. And although they threatened our lead a couple of times we were good winners in the end.

So the club were through to their first ever national cup semi-final but I must admit we were disappointed again by the draw. We felt that we could have beaten Hearts and reached the Final. Instead, we were paired with Rangers.

All I ever wanted from that game was a good performance that would make all of Scotland, and the town in particular, aware that Forfar Athletic have a future in the game.

But I almost got more than I had bargained for or dreamed of. For, after losing a goal to Derek Johnstone, we managed to equalise through Kenny Brown.

And midway through the second half the impossible happened. Left-back Brian Rankin intercepted a pass 10 yards inside our half. Off he went right to the other end and, just as he was about to be tackled, he whacked the ball past Stewart Kennedy. 2–1 to Forfar!

I'll never forget signalling across to our dug-out for a time check some minutes later. I was told there were ten minutes to go and I really believed then that we were going to make it.

We had taken everything Rangers could throw at us without caving in. I really thought we were in the Final. But with just seven minutes to go substitute Derek Parlane scored to make it 2–2.

It is history now that Alex MacDonald, Derek Johnstone and Derek Parlane added extra-time goals.

I still maintain we should have had a replay instead of that extra thirty minutes when our legs had gone. I am not saying we would have won but there would have been a lot more interest in a second meeting.

And another game would have prolonged that Indian Summer, something I'll never forget. And the whole thing proved to me that no matter how the game is going for any player he should stick at it. You never know whose turn could come next.

THE DAY THE DONS FROZE

They had kept the Premier League alive. They had played with great skill, poise and purpose. There were many to say they were an even better team than Rangers, who had won the league title. And now, for Aberdeen, it was the big day, their chance to win a top honour.

So a strike force of more than 10 000 red-bedecked Aberdeen fans travelled cheerfully to Hampden on the afternoon of 6 May 1978, to see their heroes face arch rivals Rangers in the Final of the Scottish Cup.

Aberdeen goalkeeper Bobby Clark in hot action with Rangers' Tommy McLean standing by.

There was magic about the match, a war of nerves, perhaps, for the clubs had been enjoying tremendous battles in previous games, with the Dons leading 4–2 on the League and League Cup matches already played.

Said Rangers manager Jock Wallace before the big game: 'I can't think of a final more exciting.'

Said Aberdeen manager Billy McNeill, the famous Celtic player who enjoyed a magnificent start to his managerial career at Pittodrie and who is now carrying on in that role back at Celtic: 'Everything is going well for us and we're determined to play our usual game and win the cup for these magnificent supporters of ours.

Alas for the Dons. On their day of days, they played probably their worst football of the season. They froze.

But when the Final began, there was no hint at Hampden of the sadness which was to mark Aberdeen's afternoon, with a crowd of 61 563 watching the teams line up like this:
Aberdeen: Clark, Kennedy, Ritchie, McMaster, Garner, Miller, Sullivan, Fleming, Harper, Jarvie, Davidson.
Rangers: McCloy, Jardine, Greig, Forsyth, Jackson, MacDonald, McLean, Russell, Johnstone, Smith, Cooper.
The referee was Brian McGinlay of Glasgow.

Although Aberdeen started promisingly enough, it became obvious that Rangers had pulled a master stroke. Gordon Smith had been brought back into midfield and that made all the difference. Manager Jock Wallace had remembered that the last time the teams met, Aberdeen had three players in the middle of the field against Rangers' two — and Rangers were practically skinned alive at Ibrox.

But not at Hampden. No, indeed! The Rangers switch allowed Robert Russell, that find of the season, the thin youngster who

Aberdeen's elegant Dom Sullivan.

72

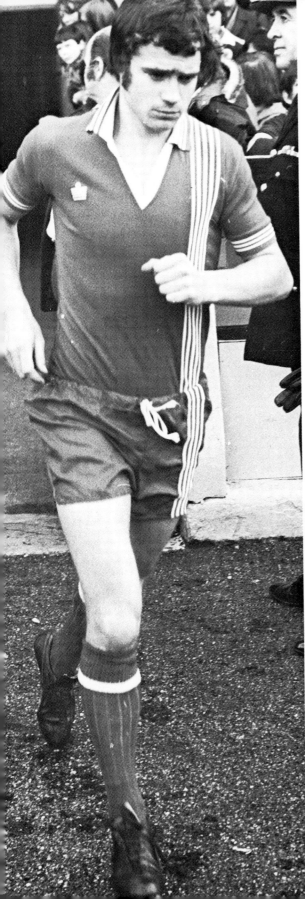

plays like Jimmy Mason or John White, to find the space he wanted. And Russell, player of the match, took command.

His passes were telling, leaving the Aberdeen players gasping. Take the opening goal for Rangers in 34 minutes. It was Russell-inspired. Tom McLean, the little right winger back in top form after a lean spell, started it by shrugging off a tackle. Then Smith and Derek Johnstone bamboozled defenders before the ball was sent out to Russell who had ghosted into an open space on the right.

Russell feinted to go to the by-line, pulled the ball back to his left foot and sent a beautiful ball into the penalty area. Alex MacDonald was first there and although he didn't connect properly his header beat Bobby Clark in the Dons goal for the vital opener.

If there was an element of luck about that one, there was only one word to describe the second, in 58 minutes – spectacular.

A high cross led to the magnificent header for which Derek Johnstone is famous. Sandy Jardine and McLean did the spadework out on the right. McLean crossed and Johnstone powered the ball past Clark.

While Aberdeen hadn't turned on the style for which they are famed, they didn't lack fight. And in 85 minutes they scored one of the most peculiar goals of the season. John McMaster at last sent over a good cross. Steve Ritchie, the new Aberdeen back from Hereford, cantered in and swung his foot at the ball which bobbled into the air, bounced off the bar, came down, and, amazingly, curled over the line.

Meanwhile, goalkeeper McCloy was swinging on the bar, believing the ball had gone over, and then wondering just what the heck had happened.

That goal made the scoreline look better for Aberdeen at 2–1, but it was by no means a true reflection of the play. Aberdeen never

Nippy Aberdeen striker Ian Fleming.

73

got a grip, never succeeded in finding their usual rhythm. Jarvie and McMaster had chances in the opening minutes it's true, but squandered them. After that, however, Rangers were seldom in trouble and won the cup easily to complete their notable treble.

Although Hampden at long last staged a Cup Final of real pomp and ceremony, turning the afternoon into a gala, the match never reached the heights – mainly because Aberdeen froze and couldn't cope with the skill and experience of Rangers.

What went wrong with Aberdeen? Why was the case of champagne carried from the foyer of Hampden Park and loaded unopened onto the bus going north after the game?

Said Aberdeen chairman Dick Donald sadly: 'It just wasn't our day. There's nothing we can say. We never really started to play.'

How could Aberdeen lose only eight matches in a fifty-game season and end up by winning nothing?

In the Final, it could have been stage fright, according to manager McNeill, who added:

'I can also point to the fact that this was my thirteenth Cup Final, obviously an unlucky one.'

Aberdeen, though, look ahead. And they have the class and talent to become one of the great Scottish sides.

They deserve great praise, anyhow, for the way they have kept competition alive in Scotland.

Rangers' Derek Johnstone goes all out in the Scottish Cup Final.

THIS MAN, GREIG

Real style, royal Rangers style, was turned on at Ibrox on Sunday, 16 April 1978, for Ibrox captain John Greig. What a day it was for John. Not only did he lead Rangers to a notable victory and score two goals against a Scotland select side, he created a new British record.

He received more than £75 000 for his testimonial, the biggest sum any British player has received.

More than 65 000 turned up to pay tribute to the inspiring skipper and on a gala day they were delighted with the entertainment provided, especially as Rangers won 5–0.

And then on 24 May John Greig was appointed manager of Rangers after Jock Wallace had resigned.

So who is this man, Greig? A tremendous enthusiast, a wit, a splendid player, one of the greatest Rangers.

And a humorist to boot, as this tale reveals. . . .

It happened on Bayview, where the fans who stand on the terracings, braving the keen cast winds from the sea and enduring the often faltering attempts of their club to regain former glories, are a pretty caustic bunch.

One bleak Saturday afternoon, then, while an East Fife player was receiving attention on the pitch at Methil after a tackle from John Greig, a grizzled spectator sourly regarded the Rangers captain, who was

John Greig scores a goal in his testimonial match against a Scotland select team at Ibrox.

Another great Scot received a deserved testimonial match last season – Pat Stanton, of Celtic. A big crowd turned up at Easter Road to see Pat, former Hibs star, in action after an anguished season in which injury had forced the stylish defender onto the sidelines.

dallying on the touchline, preparing to take a throw-in, and growled:

'Hey, Greig, I didna' ken ye were as dirty as a' that.'

John looked over his shoulder and, poker-faced, retorted: 'Have you not been watching me at all this season?'

A beard was in fashion that year for Greig, because of a face injury, and another East Fife stalwart thought he'd join in the criticism. 'Why dinna ye get a shave, Greig?' he remarked.

'You can't afford razor blades when you're only making a hundred quid a week,' said the bold Greigy.

That, to me, is the real John Greig. He's a man of the people, always quick with a quip, his patter non-stop – which may come as a surprise to those who consider he's just a hard man of football, something of a hammer-thrower, symbolizing the power so many feel is the Ibrox trademark, summed up in the story of the Rangers manager telephoning Mrs Greig to tell her: 'I'm sorry to have to let you know that John's coming home with a broken leg.' And Mrs Greig said: 'Oh, whose is it?'

Actually, that story's as old as football and the bloodcurdling tale was first told of a famous Scot, Lord Kinnaird, who captained the Wanderers and played also for Old Etonians. A flamboyant personality, was the noble lord, who wore long white trousers and a cricket cap and boasted a flaming red beard.

John Greig is flamboyant, too. Has there ever been a greater captain? I can't think of any Scot more inspiring than the man who can be a thundering dreadnought, and yet score gorgeous goals. He has lifted Rangers time and time again out of despondency by the force of his personality.

'A man of character,' I can hear ex-manager Jock Wallace booming – and if ever there was a player to fit that much abused word it's John Greig, worth his weight in gold to Rangers.

It was obvious from the start that Greig was destined to become one of the greatest Rangers. That blue shirt was tailor-made for him – although as a boy he was a Hearts supporter – for he allied to a natural footballing ability all the qualities so beloved in the marble halls of Ibrox: determination,

bravery, loyalty, tradition-consciousness, strength.

I saw him make his debut in Russia, in 1962, against Moscow Lokomotiv. John got his chance because Jim Baxter wasn't allowed to make the arduous trip to the USSR as he was needed for his Army team in the Far East. And how the crew-cut, well-built kid from Edinburgh seized that chance!

He never looked back from the day he began his first team career thousands of miles from Ibrox and on a long-grassed field under the onion-shaped domes of Moscow.

In the twilight of his playing career last season, Greig still made headlines with magnificent goals which helped Rangers to the Premier League title. But John has long been a terror of goalkeepers, with a habit of scoring goals Joe Jordan and Andy Gray dream about.

His greatest? To me, it's that superb effort against Italy at Hampden on 9 November 1965. Jim Baxter was captain of Scotland that night, Greig was at right-back.

And the Rangers pair perfected the goal that raised perhaps the greatest Hampden Roar of the century.

With 90 seconds to go in the World Cup qualifier, Baxter and Greig combined brilliantly and, with a glorious left-foot shot, John lashed the ball into the net past keeper Negri.

It was then that John Greig reached the peak of his career for after that game he was made captain of Scotland by manager Jock Stein and held the job for more than three years and a dozen internationals.

'That was one of the greatest honours I have ever been given,' says John.

What was Greig's finest victory?

'It might have been in Spain,' he feels. 'But certainly it was a time when I wasn't all that happy about being captain of Rangers.'

Rangers played Real Saragossa, whom they had defeated 2–0 in the first leg of a European Cup-Winners Cup quarter final at Ibrox.

In the tight and difficult Romereda Stadium, the Spaniards scored twice to level the score. In extra time, Rangers missed a penalty. So it came to a toss.

Greig remembers: 'It was the tensest moment in my career. I stood in the centre of the park with French referee Kitabjian and Real's skipper, Reija, with the 40 000 crowd, like myself and Reija, nervous and silent.

'To make matters worse, I had won the toss twice before in the match, at the start and before extra time was played. Could my luck hold? I doubted it but, anyhow, I decided to call "Tails". Then a silver French two-franc piece was tossed by the referee into the air, glinting in the floodlights – and was carried away by the wind.

'We three rushed to where the coin fell and the ref got there first and put his foot over it. When we were grouped together again, he lifted his foot and the right side smiled up at me. I had won the toss and we moved into the semi-final. But I was just about out for the count with the tension, I can tell you. Poor Reija was in tears. What a dreadful way a toss is to decide a big match.'

John can go on for hours about his magic moments in football with Scotland and Rangers. And there's no more entertaining companion in soccer than the voluble Greigy, who tells his tales with wit and humour.

The burly Ranger is liked by everyone in the game, which may amaze some who think opponents who have fallen after clashes with the never-say-die Greigy would gladly contribute to his retirement fund.

The truth is that Greig has been a credit to football, a man who may have played it hard but who never stooped to an underhand action, who brought drama to the game, whose enthusiasm is infectious.

He deserved his bumper benefit and he deserves his success to continue now that he has taken over the manager's role at Ibrox.

Happiness is a team called Rangers! Especially as they've just won the cup. John Greig, Peter McCloy, Derek Johnstone and Gordon Smith are certainly in gala mood here.

CONSTANTS OF SCOTTISH SOCCER

There's always a dog

Sure there is. Scottish dogs in particular appear to be great football fans. And what a waggish delight so many of them take in running onto the field and becoming part of the game.

Our four-legged friend in this picture, however, shows sound sense. It's so wet at Broomfield that he's saying to heck with the fitba', I'm going for shelter.

And Airdrie goalkeeper Davie McWilliams is obviously of the opinion he should be getting himself out of the rain as well.

There's always a character

Scottish soccer has never been short of players of character, of humour, of colour, of personality.

There was Jim Baxter of Rangers, Jimmy Brown of Kilmarnock, Charlie Tully and Tommy McInally of Celtic, Andy Kerr of Partick Thistle.

And now Ayr United have goalkeeper Hugh Sproat – yes, that's Hugh you see here, not an Indian performing a war dance – who is a great favourite with the fans.

He likes the bizarre dress. He loves to bring off the outrageous save. He prefers to be different.

But he's also a brilliant goalkeeper, a lad who's surely going places.

There's always a tragedy

Scotland has known no more dependable defender than Pat Stanton, of Celtic. Here you see the former Hibernian player coming to Celtic's rescue with a slick but cool overhead kick to avert danger, with Partick Thistle's John Marr on the spot.

But seldom a season passes in Scotland without tragedy – and it was Celtic's misfortune that Pat was out of action for most of the season because of injury.

That was one of the reasons Celtic failed to take a top honour. Stanton's calm generalling of the defence was sadly missed. Let's hope Pat and his other unlucky defensive colleague Danny McGrain, also plagued by injury, will be back at their best soon.

THE MAGIC WORLD OF THE TERRIBLE TRIO

There is, alas, only one left now, but the Terrible Trio of Tynecastle will never be forgotten. And the brilliant play of these Hearts magicians will be remembered by more than Edinburgh enthusiasts, for they were the most attractive forwards of their day – Alfie Conn, Willie Bauld and Jimmy Wardhaugh.

With the death of inside-left Jimmy Wardhaugh last season, following that of centre-forward Willie Bauld not so long before, only inside-right Alfie Conn, father of Alf of Celtic, remains of the trio whose fascinating football cast a spell over the game.

They were a nightmare to opposing defences for they had infinite resourcefulness, vivid imagination and moves as entrancing as any in the Hungarian or Brazilian handbook of soccer style. And their play was stamped with the velvet glove touch of their famous manager, Tommy Walker, also in his day a master of the inside-forward's craft.

Few could compare with the Terrible Trio. They made scoring seem easy. They bewildered defences with quicksilver pas-

The men in the middle were the Kings of Tynecastle – the Terrible Trio of Hearts, Alfie Conn, Willie Bauld and Jimmy Wardhaugh. But they wouldn't have been as famous if it hadn't been for the fine players in that great Edinburgh team. Ask your dad to name them for you. They are, from left to right, back row: Parker, McKenzie, Watters, Glidden, Dougan, Armstrong. Front row: Blackwood, Conn, Bauld, Wardhaugh, Urquhart. When did they play? In the early 50s.

sing and acute positioning. They had perfect understanding, which was not to be wondered at for they were all of the same type, quiet, modest young men, none of them a giant, but all athletic and perfectly trained and with a loyalty to club and manager which appears curious in these modern days when the thought of the huge sums to be earned in England dominates the player's mind.

And they all had flair. That is the real reason they were so magnificent. In the more ruthless organization of today's football, it isn't often we find one man with flair. To think of three gifted artists – no wonder Tynecastle fans idolized them!

Flair is a magical but elusive quality that football relentlessly pursues and seeks. Old-time Scottish stars had it in abundance – the Steels, the Masons, the Smiths, the Mortons, the McGrorys, the Walkers, the Thomsons, the Hamiltons . . . and you can go on for hours.

A few Scots of today have it – Kenny Dalglish, Alan Hansen, Don Masson, Danny McGrain, Bobby Russell – just as Jim Baxter, John White and Denis Law had it.

What is flair? England are desperately seeking it for the new team manager Ron Greenwood is building. And English managers last season tried to describe it.

As always, they had to choose Scots as the main examples. For instance, said Bob Paisley of Liverpool:

'Flair is a natural thing and it comes from someone who has something special to offer, something individual. Defenders have it too, defenders who can dispossess and create, like our lad, Alan Hansen, who we signed from Partick Thistle. He has natural aptitude and he is a centre-half with a difference. The difference is flair. And the rest of the team have to cash in on his assets. Then there's Kenny Dalglish, who is a genius at screening the ball and finding space to chip.'

Liverpool are lucky. They have two players of tremendous flair. But think of Hearts with that Terrible Trio.

Conn, Bauld and Wardhaugh considered themselves a little team within a team and that is why they always played better when they were together than when one or two of them were fielded in a Scotland side.

If these three had been playing today, they would have had manager Gordon Lee of Everton hot on their trail. Lee describes flair as great players who will express themselves for their side.

'Flair,' he says, 'is not a big centre-half pulling the ball down and beating five men in his own half when you are 2–0 down. That's stupidity. Flair is players who can do everything well but do it for the good of the team.'

Certainly Hearts' Terrible Three were unselfish players. They may have stood out as tremendous individualists but always they worked for the side.

And that pleased Bill Shankly, former manager of Liverpool, who defines flair like this:

'Flair is vision. It is like a great chess player – a man in advance of anyone else, thinking quicker than anyone else. Denis Law is the supreme example.

'Sometimes we think of flair as trickery. Tommy Finney had trickery but he also had the vision to merge his cleverness into normal patterns. He was an individual but he made sure it never hurt his side. He was always part of a side.

'And that's why Conn, Wardhaugh and Bauld were so great. They were all masters, skilled and strong. But they didn't just work for each other. They made sure that their flair worked for the whole Hearts team.'

The Terrible Three brought out a new approach to Scottish football. They combined the grace of the old style with methods which were just starting to find favour in Europe. Willie Bauld, for example, was the most intelligent centre-

forward in the land. Traditionalists criticized him for his novel leadership. Like the great Hungarian, Hidegkuti, he lay deep. Yet any goalkeeper of the day would have told you ruefully that Willie was a devastatingly accurate marksman, especially with that flashing, fair head.

Bauld, an Edinburgh lad, was always a fanatical Hearts supporter – but the club almost missed him. Sunderland signed him when he was an outstanding junior with Muesselburgh Athletic. Much to the relief of Hearts, the signing was not in order and it had to be cancelled.

Willie returned to the Athletic, then joined Newtongrange Star. In 1946 Hearts woke up to the fact that here was a centre-forward with a golden future and they signed him. For a season he was loaned to Edinburgh City, and did so well that he was soon called up to Tynecastle.

Willie experienced many joyous football moments, but he had bitterness too. Playing for Scotland against England at Hampden, he hit the ball against the bar. It was a historic miss. If he had scored Scotland might have gone to Rio to play in the World Cup.

But the people who remember this miss and criticize forget conveniently that Bauld made a gallant attempt to place the ball out of the England goalkeeper's reach.

The most elegant of the trio was Jimmy Wardhaugh, who died soon after he had stepped out of the Hearts bus on the way back from a match with East Fife at Methil.

Wardhaugh came from Berwick and once there was confusion when he was chosen for a Scottish international team, some officials imagining he was English. But no-one was prouder than Jimmy to be a Scot and play for his country. His clever manoeuvres on the ball delighted Tynecastle fans and class was stamped on every move.

Jimmy Wardhaugh, that fine inside-left, at the peak of his career.

You could trace the Tommy Walker influence on Wardhaugh's play – the same grace, the same eel-like wriggle. Jimmy was well trained in avoiding opponents – he played Rugby at school.

The other member of the Terrible Trio is Alfie Conn, who was the burliest of the three. He was, in the words of the fans, 'a real hard grafter' and his strength was a paramount feature in blending the Terrible Trio. But Alfie, like Dave McKay and so many others who are alleged to be merely hard players, had splendid skills and his support provided the solid framework on which the pretty Hearts patterns were woven.

Long ago, I remember writing: 'They are a trio of distinction, each in his own right a player in the £20 000 class. Together ... well, Hearts fans say all the money in the Bank of England couldn't buy them.'

I wonder what they would be worth today if they were still playing? They would, naturally, have to be transferred as a trio. Would a million pounds be paid? Conn, Bauld and Wardhaugh would have been well worth that sum.

One thing's for sure – in their heyday the Terrible Trio made football a magical world.

Moment of glory for Willie Bauld, holding aloft the League Cup won by Hearts all those years ago. Behind him is team-mate Bobby Parker, now a Tynecastle director.

PLAYER OF THE YEAR
Dandy Derek
Wins a Double

Dandy Derek Johnstone, Rangers' ace striker, was Scotland's Player of the Year last season – twice.

The man who makes scoring look so easy was chosen first by the Scottish football writers and then by his fellow professionals as their No.1. And it was good to see an exciting attacker take the honours for, in recent years, the honours list has hardly been dominated by strikers.

Curiously, Derek could be called the reluctant striker, for despite his outstanding goal-grabbing ability in the air and on the ground, he still fancies himself as a centre-half. He's pretty good in that position, too, but as an attacker he's worth his weight in gold to Scotland and Rangers for he has the knack of scoring goals from half-chances.

Derek Johnstone, born in Dundee in 1953, won international honours as an Under-15 schoolboy and was quickly whisked south to Ibrox by Rangers, who pipped many other senior clubs.

And what a spectacular start Derek made with Rangers. He scored twice on his debut, when he was only 16, in a league match against Cowdenbeath at Ibrox in 1970 and followed up by netting the winner in his second match – the League Cup Final in which Rangers beat Celtic 1–0.

After that stupendous start to his career at Ibrox, Derek progressed year by year, winning all honours at home with Rangers, plus a European Cup Winners Cup medal and

Brilliant striker Derek Johnstone in action.

caps at youth, Under-23 and full Scotland level. He has made more than 360 appearances for Rangers and scored more than 150 goals.

Although he's big, Derek is sure-footed and fast and no player in the country times his jump better.

Well, once Scotland was famed for her outstanding forwards, but since the Player of the Year award was first made in 1965, there has been only one other attacker honoured –

Gordon Wallace, of Raith Rovers, in 1967–68. All the others have been defenders, plus a few midfield men.

At the age of 25, Derek is really only starting what must be one of the most glittering careers any Scottish player has known.

But it's not all glamour being a successful striker. Front-rank footballers take many knocks and here Derek Johnstone receives treatment from Rangers' physiotherapist, Tom Craig.

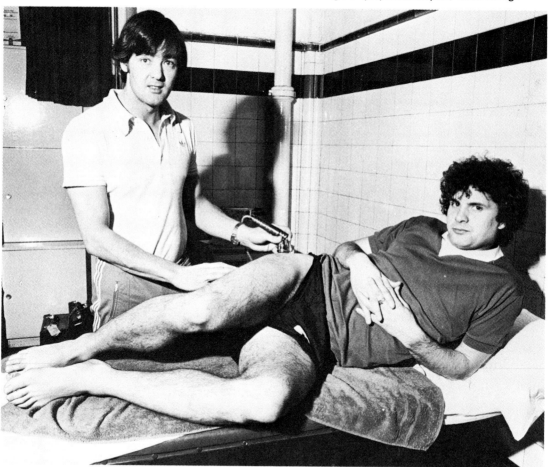

THE RIGHT ROAD IS THE ROAD NORTH
by Steve Ritchie

I allow myself a quiet chuckle every time I read a newspaper report about a Scottish player saying he has to go to England to be successful, because I have learned from experience that being attached to an English League side does not guarantee fame and fortune.

It is great if you happen to be with Manchester United, Liverpool or Leeds. That way you are sure of being in the public eye most of the time. Players like Kenny Dalglish, Gordon McQueen and Joe Jordan have made it really big down south and there is no way I am going to argue with that.

But my experience has shown that some players can do far better in their own backyard.

As a youngster I tried my luck with Bristol City but I couldn't settle down there and returned to Scotland with Morton. A couple of years later I got another chance to sample football in the south with Hereford United. To be honest, I enjoyed my football at Hereford for quite a long time and, in fact, helped them to win promotion. But things started to go wrong for me in the next season when the club brought in another left-back and I found myself out of the team.

That's how it was last March. There I was sitting in the reserve side as the first team slipped further and further down the League towards a return to the Fourth Division. I don't think I had ever been so depressed with my career in football. The club seemed to have no ambition and I appeared to be at a dead-end.

Then suddenly one day I was called into the manager's office for a conversation that caused my life to take an unexpected upswing.

It transpired that Aberdeen manager Billy McNeill had remembered me as a Morton player and had kept track of me in England. He had made an enquiry about a possible transfer and the boss wanted to know if I would be prepared to move.

I didn't have to be asked twice. I was out of Hereford so quickly that I didn't even get a chance to say goodbye to my team-mates. I

95

don't know how they felt about my move but I can guess that they would have been just as keen if the chance had been offered to them.

I didn't know immediately, of course, just how good a move I had made ... but I soon found out. For moving to Pittodrie was a real breath of fresh air and I realized that almost the first time I walked in the main door.

It doesn't take long to know when you are with a club that is determined to be successful. I quickly learned that everything that goes on at Pittodrie is geared to success.

For instance, they have led the way in making the supporters comfortable. They have one of the best stadiums anywhere in Britain and they are always looking for ways of improving facilities.

It didn't take me long, either, to realize that the players, the manager and the coaches are all ambitious for success. And what a great bunch they make. There are no cliques. It is a matter of everyone doing his best for the club. They made me feel at home immediately and I quickly learned that they have some really good players.

As it turned out my arrival in March came at almost the best possible time, for the club were still involved in the League and in the Scottish Cup. Just after I came to Pittodrie I found myself involved in a series of vital matches, although it is history now that we just failed in both competitions.

Failure or not I shall certainly never forget that run-in at the end of last season. I think, in fact, that I was so keen to repay the club's faith in me that I didn't play to my best form.

But I was grateful to be part of the team at that exciting time. A few weeks after my career seemed dead, I was playing at Hampden in the Scottish Cup semi-final against Partick Thistle, my first game at Scotland's home of football.

I enjoyed the experience, particularly as we won 4–2 that night. That meant we were back at Hampden for the Final, although we had to concentrate on league games for the next couple of weeks.

We managed to push Rangers all the way for that Premier League title even though it went to Ibrox on the last day of the league season.

The following week we met them in the Cup Final and again they just got the better of us. We didn't play nearly as well as we can but it was an unforgettable experience for me in two ways.

Firstly, I got the Aberdeen goal which, if it had come earlier, could have seen us produce a real fight-back.

Secondly, as I collected my runners-up medal, I felt convinced that I am with a club which is good enough and ambitious enough to compete for all the honours in the future.